Hope in every Season! ♡ Michele

Hope
In All Seasons

Devotional Readings to
Encourage You
in Every Season of Life

By Steve and Marjie Schaefer

ISBN: 979-8-9900034-0-8

Cover Design: Lisa McKenney

Interior Layout and Design: Kristi Knowles

To our beloved children and grandchildren:

Hayley, Jordan, Rachael, Matthew, Luke, Jack, and Indie.

May you always cling to the One who will always be your Living Hope.

Now may the God of hope fill you with all joy and peace in believing, that you may abound in hope by the power of the Holy Spirit.

Romans 15:13

Table of Contents

Introduction

Why *Hope*? Because Marjie and I are convinced the world has lost its collective mind! And if you doubt this, please feel free to stop at this point and scroll through the latest headlines from all your news feeds. Still doubting? No wonder our society is suffering from an unprecedented and escalating mental health crisis. Depression and anxiety are seemingly out of control for so many. And yet, with so much darkness and fearmongering bombarding us day in and day out, in my not-too-distant past I had a well-meaning colleague tell me, "Steve, hope is not a strategy."

While I appreciate the need to embrace a comprehensive roadmap to achieve stated objectives, in hindsight I believe we were operating with two very two different definitions of this one word. Hers seemed to be more like wishful thinking, akin to knocking on wood or crossing one's fingers. My definition of hope, on the other hand, was quite different. It was (and remains) a much more fixed, certain, and guaranteed outcome in what I believe. A hope not impacted by the shifting sands of time, another loss by my favorite sports team, or the whim of the latest leader or fad. Truly, it's a hope that can only be found in the Bible. A living hope that declares, "We will win!" because Jesus won. A hope that enables us to walk as victors and overcomers, reigning in life, because all authority in heaven and earth has been given to the One who alone reigns, our Lord and Savior Jesus Christ. His finished work on the cross is the basis of this, our Christian hope. No matter how dark, bleak, and dismal things may look in our lives or in our world, we know how our story—and how *the* story—ends. Walking by faith and not by sight, regardless of how loud our circumstances may be screaming at us, the Bible is our true north. For ultimately, this living hope points us not to something, but to Someone. While all our earthly hopes will ultimately come to a disappointing end, Jesus Christ will not. He is alive, and because He lives, we can face both today and tomorrow. With great hope!

And why *Seasons*? Well, as we all know, on an annual basis we experience four distinct seasons, especially if you are adequately removed from both the equator and either of the two poles. And so, these tangible weather patterns we experience are both astronomical and meteorological in their origin. And to quantify all of this, in October of 1582, the bulk of humanity adopted the Gregorian calendar (thank you Pope Gregory XIII) as the means by which we would mark and monitor these seasonal changes. With that as a background, Marjie and I believe God has given us these seasons as a metaphorical paradigm for living and understanding the Christian life. Like seasonal changes in our climate, in life we also have ebbs and flows. We have ups, and we have downs. We have the sunny seasons of SUMMER where we are center-stage, and light, life, and fruit abound. And then the FALL of transition occurs, whether that transition be forced or volitional, and what was once so bountiful, now seems to be in decline and fading away. In this season, we may feel as though we're being put on the bench, as it were. Then the dark days of WINTER set in, and with them comes apparent loss, anonymity, obscurity, and concealment. Stripped of visible fruit, doubt often sets in, and we wonder: Have I, like the trees in WINTER, become temporarily bare, or am I now permanently barren? By God's grace, He provides the answer to this question with the season of SPRING, when life returns, and the dance begins anew. While the weather patterns of creation have a fairly consistent annual rhythm, the seasons of life are more apt to be very inconsistent in length. Whereas some seasons in life can be measured in terms of days, weeks, and months, I suspect most seasons we experience are years in their duration.

Regardless of the season you find yourself in as you peruse these short devotional readings, may you be encouraged in your faith, for you the believer can always have hope in every season of life.

SPRING

God loves each of us as if there was only one of us.
Saint Augustine

Christ is love covered over in flesh.
Thomas Goodwin

Relationship

Marjie's favorite season is SUMMER. I, on the other hand, love SPRING. After four plus months of darkness, gray, and rain (with a sprinkle of some Seattle snow-panic thrown in here and there), I'm ready for warmth, sunshine, light, and longer days. I am more than happy to sacrifice one hour of sleep to daylight savings so I can begin to enjoy those lighted evenings. And to cap off this blessed time of the year, April showers do in fact bring May flowers. Flowers blossom and the trees shoot forth their colorful leaves in this glorious month. All creation is abuzz, displaying its beauty as it once again declares the glory of its Creator. Amidst the hustle and bustle of life, it's in May when I love to pause and soak in the radiance of its vibrant beauty. So as far as I'm concerned, all is right with the world in SPRING .

How appropriate in this season of new beginnings we celebrate Easter. Lost and separated from God because of our sin, mankind's only hope would be if God initiated and intervened into the affairs of humanity, for *"There is none righteous, no, not one. There is none who does good, no, not one. For all have sinned and fallen short of the glory of God"* (Romans 3:10, 12, 23). No amount of human effort could ever have bridged this infinite gap between God and man. Our only hope would be divine intervention. Him coming to us. And intervene He did in the person of Jesus Christ. An intervention that establishes first a relationship with God, so we, in turn, might establish loving relationships with each other. For as Jesus clearly declared, the greatest commandment has everything to do with relationships:

> *"'You shall love the Lord your God with all your heart, with all your soul, and with all your mind.' This is the first and great commandment. And the second is like it: 'You shall love your neighbor as yourself'"* (Matthew 22:37-39).

Reconciled vertically first to God, and then horizontally with our neighbors. This is the power of the cross and the resurrected life, *"For He made Him who knew no sin to be sin for us, that we might become the righteousness of God in Him"* (2 Corinthians 5:21). *"We love because He first loved us"* (1 John 4:19). Experience the love of the Father in Christ His Son, then love people. Life and living at its essence.

Blessed Assurance

"And He said to him, "Truly, I say to you, today you will be with me in Paradise"(Luke 23:43).

At the center of every SPRING lies the center of human history, and the solitary portal through Whom we may enter into relationship with the Living God. So, let's begin by spending these first few days reflecting on the cross of Jesus Christ. Specifically, the final words of Christ spoken from the cross.

In the passage above we hear Christ's response to one of the two thieves. The one who, in his final moments before death, repented of his failed life and issued a desperate cry of faith, *"Lord, remember me when You come into Your kingdom."* Here we see how grace works. The wonder of the gospel on display. For thieves and criminals. For doctors, accountants, baristas, and car mechanics. For you and me. Bringing nothing to the table but our empty hands, Christ freely lavishes His love upon the objects of His affection.

Our eternal destiny is not determined by the life we have lived or the sins we have committed. It is purely based on simple trust in Christ and His grace. Nothing more is required. We cannot add to it, and we can take nothing from it. *"For by grace you have been saved through faith, and that not of yourselves, it is the gift of God"* (Ephesians 2:8). Jesus told His disciples He was returning to His Father's house to prepare a place for them, and now this promise included a dying thief with not a single good deed to His name. This is the gift of salvation, and this is the assurance of salvation. And for believers with potentially more time here on earth, with a slight change of punctuation, this assurance is no less resolute, *"Truly, I say to you today, you will be with me in Paradise."*

Tangible Forgiveness

"Jesus said, 'Father, forgive them, for they know not what they do'"
(Luke 23:34).

Jesus has just come from a sham trial, survived incredible amounts of torture, hangs naked on a wooden cross suffering excruciating pain, and is on exhibition before a jeering, mocking crowd. The pain is so severe that Roman soldiers were known to cut out the tongues of their victims to shut their loud screams of agony. And yet, in this context, Jesus offers up a prayer. A prayer of forgiveness. A prayer for the Roman soldiers who were executing Him, for Pilate and Herod who chose not to stop this sentence of death, for the crazed mob who shouted, "Crucify Him!", and for His scattered disciples who were nowhere to be found in His final hours. And it was a prayer for you and me.

Earlier in His ministry, Jesus taught about forgiveness. And in His teachings, He told His followers to go beyond no longer holding an offense, harboring a grudge, or clinging to resentment against another person or persons. He said, *"Love your enemies, do good to those who hate you, bless those who curse you, pray for those who abuse you"* (Luke 6:27-28). Here, on the cross, Jesus was now practicing what He had preached. In the ultimate display of love this world has ever known, Jesus shed His blood for those who hated, cursed, and abused Him. Here we see our path for true and complete reconciliation with others. While it begins with forgiveness, its conclusion is never complete until we too can show tangible expressions of love towards those we once regarded as enemies.

Paid in Full

"When Jesus had received the sour wine, He said, 'It is finished!' And bowing His head, He gave up His spirit" (John 19:30).

Seven hundred years earlier, the prophet Isaiah wrote the Messiah would bear our griefs, carry our sorrows, be wounded for our transgressions, bruised for our iniquities, chastised for our peace, and scourged for our healing. Now so many centuries later, Jesus fulfills all of these on the cross by uttering one final word, *"tetelestai"*. This word means *to end; to bring to completion; to conclude, to accomplish; to fulfill; or to finish.* In ancient times, when a servant was sent on a mission and later returned to his master, he would say, *"Tetelestai,"* meaning, *"I have done exactly what you requested"* or *"The mission is now accomplished."* In business, when a debt had been fully paid off, the parchment on which the debt was recorded was stamped with *Tetelestai,* which meant the debt had been paid in full.

And so, if you are consumed with grief, remember Jesus bore your grief. If you are overwhelmed with sorrows, remember He carried your sorrows. If you are trapped in a life of transgression, remember He was wounded for your transgressions. If you are living in sin, you can be forgiven because He was bruised for your iniquities. If you are tormented and have no peace, remember He was chastised for your peace. And if you are physically sick, remember He was scourged for your healing. As the hymn says,

"Jesus paid it all,
all to Him I owe,
sin had left a crimson stain,
He washed it white as snow."

He's Still Showing Up

"He is not here: for He is risen, as He said"
(Matthew 28:6).

Easter is a day in which we mark and celebrate the fact of Jesus Christ's resurrection from the dead and His appearance to His disciples and followers. He appeared to Mary Magdalene who was suffering in her grief, *"But Mary stood outside by the tomb weeping, and as she wept, she stooped down and looked into the tomb"* (John 20:11). He appeared to Thomas, the one who doubted, *"Unless I see in His hands the print of the nails, and put my finger into the print of the nails, and put my hand into His side, I will not believe"* (John 20:25). And He appeared to Peter, the one who had failed Him not once, but three times, *"Then he began to curse and swear, saying, 'I do not know the Man!'"* (Matthew 26:74).

Because He is alive, and because He never changes, Jesus is still showing up to those who weep, to those who doubt, and to those who have failed Him. So, if you have pain, if you have questions, and if you have blown it, then Jesus wants to meet you right where you're at. There is *"healing in His wings"* (Malachi 4:2), and *"a bruised reed He will not break"* (Isaiah 42:3). Meaning the very things we think alienate ourselves from God, are actually the very things that endear God to His children. Your frailties and deficiencies do not repel Jesus, but rather attract Him to you. So let Easter be a reminder—Jesus is still showing up, just as you are, to those He died and rose for.

He Sees You

"Thereafter, Hagar used another name to refer to the Lord, who had spoken to her. She said, 'You are the God who sees me.' She also said, "Have I truly seen the one who sees me?"' (Genesis 16:13).

Abandoned and treated harshly by those closest to her, a pregnant Hagar fled alone into the wilderness. On her own and in the desert, she had nowhere to go. In this lonely state of invisibility, the *"Angel of the Lord"* sees her and comes to her. In fact, He not only comes to her, but calls her by name, *"Hagar, Sarai's maid, where have you come from, and where are you going?"* (Genesis 16:8). And she, called by name and no longer alone, in return calls God *"Lahai Roi",* The God Who Sees.

Lahai Roi is not blind to your plight. While you may feel invisible in this world, you are not unseen to Him, the One who will never abandon you. He comes to you and calls you too by name. And as with Hagar, He will seek you out and arrive at the moment of your greatest need. Sometimes early, but never late. God sees you in your heartache, pain, confusion, and suffering. And when you feel abandoned and at your lowest, feeling like no one cares about you or your predicaments, know and believe He does. Come to Him, and He'll meet you in your downcast state and pour out fresh grace and love upon you, His dearly beloved child.

How Big is Your God?

"Oh, magnify the Lord with me, and let us exalt His name together"
(Psalm 34:3).

Looking back over our thirty-six-year marriage, there was a space of about four years where Marjie and I really struggled. Not with our relationship or our marriage, but with the onslaught of problems we were facing. Problems which came at us from every angle. For what seemed like hours each day, we would talk about the latest problem and what we should do to resolve it. It seemed like the barrage would never end. Fortunately, at our lowest point, Marjie pulled an unread book off the shelf called "Fresh Faith" by Jim Cymbala, and God used it to begin restoring us back to life, and to our faith in our great God.

In hindsight, we had regressed to talking about the problems, which in essence magnified and exalted them, which in turn decreased our faith and shrank our God. We had very big problems with a tiny little God. When David wrote verse three above, he wasn't insinuating we need to make God larger than He actually is—like a magnifying glass would do with small print. What he was saying is when we praise the Lord with our mouths *("I will bless the Lord at all times; His praise shall continually be in my mouth"* Psalm 34:1.) we draw nearer to Him, and when we do, He becomes larger to us. Our faith grows. And isn't that what we need? A big view of God? Don't we all have big problems, worries, and concerns? Of course we do. And that is exactly why we need to magnify and exalt God with our mouths (in worship and in speech) so we can see Him for who He truly is.

The Hawthorne Effect

"Then Jesus spoke to them again, saying, 'I am the light of the world.
He who follows Me shall not walk in darkness,
but have the light of life'" (John 8:12).

"For you were once darkness, but now you are light in the Lord.
Walk as children of light" (Ephesians 5:8).

From 1924-1932, in Cicero, Illinois, a Western Electric plant by the name of *Hawthorne Works*, commissioned a study to gauge the impact of worker productivity by introducing an array of variables in the workplace. To the bewilderment of the researchers, the workers' productivity improved whenever any change (positive or negative) was made. The Hawthorne Effect, coined by Henry A. Landsberger in 1958 when analyzing these experiments years later, is the positive response in which individuals modify an aspect of behavior in reaction to their awareness of being observed. Landsberger suggested the novelty of increased attention and interest being shown in them created the motivation they needed to improve their personal performance.

When Adam and Eve sinned, Genesis says they *"hid themselves from the presence of the Lord God"* (Genesis 3:8), and shame has been with us ever since. By God's grace, Jesus took our shame and *"endured the cross, despising the shame, and has sat down at the right hand of the throne of God"* (Hebrews 12:2). So no longer do we need to hide from Him. In Christ, He sees us and loves us. Warts and all. Every hour of every day, He gives you His undivided attention and is incredibly interested in your interests. So yes, we are being watched. But these are the eyes of love on the objects of His affection. Like a smiling mom or dad watching their young child laugh and play in the park. So, in response, let's walk in His light and love. Why? Because He first loved us.

Mind the Gap

"Trust in the Lord with all your heart,
and lean not on your own understanding;
in all your ways acknowledge Him,
and He shall direct your path" (Proverbs 3:5-6).

If you've ever traveled to the UK and ridden on their subway system, you've seen the sign "Mind The Gap" everywhere you went. Roughly translated, it means "Watch out for the space between the train and the platform!" Gaps between platforms and trains can be very dangerous, and so can the gaps we have in our own lives. Between what is, and what we wish it to be. The gap between the circumstances we're in, and the circumstances we desire. Between the beliefs or behaviors of a loved one, and what we want to see in them. The gap between our prayers, and the apparent lack of response to them. Or maybe it's the answer we did receive, versus the answer we really wanted.

These spaces in life are hard to manage, especially if you excel at solving problems. The natural human response is to jump in and try to fix these gaps. In its best form we attempt to problem-solve, and at its worst, we try and control or manipulate the situation or person in our life. Unfortunately, living in the microwave culture as we do, patience and waiting are not exactly coveted virtues anymore. And so, what do we do with these gaps? In all of them, the Lord is asking us the same question, "Do you trust Me?" Whether our responsibility with the gap is somewhere between waiting patiently or jumping in to resolve, His question to us remains, "Do you trust Me?" So today, let's take inventory of the gaps we all have, and believe along with David, *"The Lord is trustworthy in all He promises, and faithful in all He does"* (Psalm 145:13).

Dwelling In Us Richly

"Let the word of Christ dwell in you richly in all wisdom, teaching and admonishing one another in psalms and hymns and spiritual songs, singing with grace in your hearts to the Lord" (Colossians 3:16).

Recently I read fascinating research showing minimal to no impact in a person's life if they read the Bible three or less times per week, but reading it four or more days made all the difference in the world. This would confirm Colossians 3:16, that when the Word dwells in us richly, good things happen. As Jesus said, *"It is written, man shall not live by bread alone, but by every word that proceeds from the mouth of God"* (Matthew 4:4). Why? Because, unlike anything else ever written, *"..the word of God is living and powerful..."* (Hebrews 4:12).

So, what does it mean to "dwell in us richly"? I think of my own home, and how I happen to dwell in it. During the workweek, I would say I "dwell in it quickly." In the morning, I quickly enter the kitchen to get my coffee, rush through my bathroom routine, throw on my clothes in the bedroom, and then jump in my car and I'm off. But on the weekend, it's a different story. As I putter around the house, I would say I "dwell in it richly." Over the course of the weekend, each room is typically accessed, this thing or that thing fixed or cleaned, and the yard routinely attended to in some form or fashion. In like manner, this is how the Word is to be in us, mimicking our weekend (vs. weekday) dwelling experience. And if it does, over the course of time, we will experience the life, power, and hope of the Scriptures, for in the Bible we will find the person of Jesus. As He said, *"You search the Scriptures because you think they give you eternal life. But the Scriptures point to me!"* (John 5:39-40). And as we draw near to Him, He promises to draw near to us.

Another Bad News Day

*"Though the fig tree may not blossom, nor fruit be on the vines;
though the labor of the olive may fail, and the fields yield no food;
though the flock may be cut off from the fold, and there be no herd
in the stalls--yet I will rejoice in the Lord, I will joy in the God of my
salvation. The Lord God is my strength; He will make my feet like
deer's feet, and He will make me walk on my high hills"
(Habakkuk 3:17-19).*

These days, every day, it seems like the one certainty we can count on is a bad news day. The constant 24/7 news feeds, with their 24-hour news cycles, create a relentless barrage of negativity and fear that can depress our souls, causing us to be discouraged and to dread what may lie ahead. And yet, as the writer of Ecclesiastes said, *"there is nothing new under the sun."* Like us, the prophet Habakkuk found himself in a similar predicament 2,600+ years ago. So fed up with the bad news and the evil of his day, he cried out in complaint to God and basically said, "Do something!" God obliged, and in essence said, "Ok, I'll do something. I'll raise up the Chaldeans who will destroy your nation." The news for Habakkuk just went from bad to worse.

Or did it? From a human perspective, of course it did. But something inside Habakkuk changed. Something clicked. Rather than being emotionally tossed around by what he saw and heard, he began stepping away from all that discouraging noise and started looking up. With eyes of faith, he looked away from what he once feared and looked to the One who was truly in control. The Lord was in charge, and no matter what happened down here, Habakkuk's faith in that would no longer be shaken by current events and the news feeds of his day. As it was back then, so it is today. No matter what happens in this crazy world of ours, we too can rejoice in the Lord and find joy in the God of our salvation.

The Why

"For by grace you have been saved through faith,
and that not of yourselves; it is the gift of God,
not of works, lest anyone should boast" (Ephesians 2:8-9).

Try as you might, you will not find one thing for you to do in Ephesians 1, 2, or 3. All three chapters are devoted to indicative statements, or statements of fact. These declarations require not obedience, but belief. If I say, "the sky is blue", there is nothing for you to do, but there is something for you to either believe or not believe. Now unfortunately, as adults, we seem to have a natural proclivity to jump right to the "do and don't" checklist, having lost our childhood curiosity of wanting to know the *why* of life. But without a solid faith in the *why* (Ephesians 1-3), the *what* (Ephesians 4-6) will become an unbearable burden too heavy to lift, for religion is a condemning taskmaster. For this reason, Ephesians 1-3 is a wonderful place to anchor down and spend considerable time reflecting on, and believing in, the finished work of God.

He tells us:

"we have been adopted...we are now accepted in the Beloved... He's sealed us with the Holy Spirit of promise, who is the guarantee of our inheritance...He has made us alive...God, who is rich in mercy because of His great love with which He loved us, raised us up that in the ages to come He might show the exceeding riches of His grace in His kindness towards us in Christ Jesus....in Christ we have boldness and access with confidence through faith in Him...that we would comprehend what is the width and length and depth and height—to know the love of Christ which passes knowledge....now to Him who is able to do exceedingly, abundantly above all that we ask or think, according to the power that works in us, to Him be glory in the church by Christ Jesus to all generations, forever and ever. Amen."

Who are you?

"Jesus, knowing that the Father had given all things into His hands, and that He had come from God and was going to God, rose from supper and laid aside His garments, took a towel and girded Himself. After that, he poured water into a basin and began to wash the disciples' feet"
(John 13:3-5).

Oxford's definition of the word *identity* is "the fact of being who or what a person is." In essence, the real you. In the passage above, we have what I believe are the best identity verses in the Bible and what supernaturally manifests when you believe who you really are in Christ. Jesus knew who He was, and that awareness enabled Him to serve others. How about you? Who are you? If you are a Christian, then Galatians 2:20 describes your identity:

"I have been crucified with Christ; it is no longer I who live, but Christ lives in me; and the life which I now live in the flesh I live by faith in the Son of God, who loved me and gave Himself for me."

Christ in you is your new identity. If anyone is a Christian, they are a new creation. For if you are in Christ, God says: You are chosen, holy, blameless, alive, free, beloved, adopted, accepted, redeemed, forgiven, and have eternal purpose. You are who God says you are. Believing Him will empower you to love and serve others just as Jesus did.

Identity theft is real. Don't let people, the world, your past, circumstances, or the devil try and rob you of the new identity God has given you in Christ. For *"In Christ dwells all the fullness of the Godhead bodily, and you are complete in Him"* (Colossians 2:9-10).

The Fundamentals

"And now these three remain: faith, hope, and love.
But the greatest of these is love" (1 Corinthians 13:13).

In July of 1961, after a heartbreaking loss in the NFL Championship game the prior season, Vince Lombardi opened training camp for his Green Bay Packers in an unusual way. After all the players sat down, the coach held up a football and said, "Gentlemen, this is a football!" These grizzled veterans of the game were then told to turn to page one of their playbooks, where they would focus on the fundamentals of the game for the rest of camp—blocking, tackling, throwing, and catching. They would go on to win the NFL Championship game that season.

In the same way, when life deals a heartbreaking blow as it will often do, I have found it helpful, and in fact quite necessary, to always keep returning to the fundamentals of who I am and what I believe as a follower of Christ. In that spirit, I offer the following from God's Word:

Faith: *"He [Abraham] did not waver at the promise of God through unbelief, but was strengthened in faith, giving glory to God, and being fully convinced that what He had promised He was also able to perform"* (Romans 4:20-21).

Hope: *"Now may the God of hope fill you with all joy and peace in believing, that you may abound in hope by the power of the Holy Spirit"* (Romans 15:13).

Love: *"Beloved, let us love one another, for love is of God; and everyone who loves is born of God and knows God. He who does not love does not know God, for God is love. In this the love of God was manifested toward us, that God has sent His only begotten Son into the world, that we might live through Him. In this is love, not that we loved God, but that He loved us and sent His Son to be the propitiation for our sins. Beloved, if God so loved us, we also ought to love one another"* (1 John 4:7-11).

A Solid Foundation

*"Therefore whoever hears these sayings of Mine, and does them,
I will liken him to a wise man who built his house on the rock:
and the rain descended, the floods came, and the winds blew and
beat on that house; and it did not fall, for it was founded on the
rock" (Matthew 7:24-25).*

The foundation of a home is not exciting, beautiful, or glamorous. You've probably never had a real estate agent excited to show you (on hands and knees) how fabulous the foundation is when touring a home. And you've never seen HGTV devote a series or even a show to the best home foundations in America. While the granite counter tops, new paint, and furniture get all the glory, the poor, mundane foundation lives in relative anonymity. And yet, with a crumbling foundation, the glitz and bling grabbing the headlines of a home are, in the end, meaningless. That home is in need of bulldozing.

In the above passage, beyond *where* you build your foundation (rock vs. sand), Jesus lays out two principles about building a solid foundation for your life. The first is that you must both hear and do the sayings of Jesus. *Hears* (or reads) implies Biblical literacy, and the word *do* is an action, a verb. Both are required to have a foundation built on a rock. More on that over the next couple days. The second principle is *when* the foundation is built. It's built *before* the rain, floods, and winds come. Trying to lay a solid foundation when a Cat 5 hurricane is bearing down upon you is not a good time start. Counterintuitively, the best time to lay a solid foundation is when there is no apparent need to do so, such as when Noah labored for years building an ark on dry land in the desert. How foolish he must have seemed to his neighbors.

A Solid Foundation (continued)

"Therefore, whoever hears these sayings of Mine, and does them, I will liken him to a wise man who built his house on the rock: and the rain descended, the floods came, and the winds blew and beat on that house; and it did not fall, for it was founded on the rock"
(Matthew 7:24-25).

William Randolph Hearst invested a fortune collecting art treasures from around the world. One day Hearst read the description of a valuable art item which he sent his agent abroad to find. After months of searching, the agent reported he had finally found the treasure. To the surprise of Hearst, the priceless masterpiece was stored in none other than his own warehouse. The multi-millionaire had been searching all over the world for a treasure he already possessed. Had he only read the catalogue of his treasures, he would have saved himself a lot of time and money.

We too, like Mr. Hearst, possess priceless riches found in our catalogue of treasures, the Bible. In Christ, the promises in the Bible are ours as part of our inheritance as an adopted son or daughter. And so, before we can *do* the sayings of Jesus, we first have to *hear* (or in our case, read) the sayings of Jesus. As we read the Bible and begin to believe and trust what He has said, we begin to discover just how wealthy we really are and just how many masterpieces we really own. And when we come to this realization, we too, like the psalmist, will declare:

> *"Therefore I love your commandments more than gold, yes, than fine gold! The law of Your mouth is better to me than thousands of coins of gold and silver. I rejoice at Your word as one who finds great treasure"* (Psalm 119: 72, 127, 162).

A Solid Foundation (continued)

"Therefore, whoever hears these sayings of Mine, and does them, I will liken him to a wise man who built his house on the rock: and the rain descended, the floods came, and the winds blew and beat on that house; and it did not fall, for it was founded on the rock"
(Matthew 7:24-25).

Hetty Green died in 1916 with a fortune estimated to be $200 million. In today's dollars, that would be $5.76 BILLION. She was rich but lived like a miser. She never used hot water or turned on the heat. She wore the same black dress and underwear every day until they wore out. She heated her oatmeal on a radiator. Her son Ned broke his leg, and when she refused medical care, he developed gangrene and eventually had to have his leg amputated. In the end, when she determined a $150 dollar hernia operation was too expensive, she chose to live in misery until her death.

Hetty knew she was rich, but lived as though she was poor. In our spiritual lives, the Bible would call this "unbelief"—when you know the riches of God's Word but act contrary to it. James issued the same warning when he said, *"But be doers of the Word, and not hearers only, deceiving yourselves"* (James 1:22). So, in the end, Hetty becomes an example of what building your house on sand looks like. And so does Mr. Hearst, who failed to even read about the catalogue of treasures he owned. No, to build your house on the solid rock of Christ, according to Matthew 7:24-25, we'll need to both hear *and* do.

From the hymn *How Firm a Foundation:*

> *How firm a foundation, ye saints of the Lord,*
> *Is laid for your faith in His excellent Word!*
> *What more can He say than to you He hath said,*
> *To you, who for refuge to Jesus have fled?*

Flying By Instruments

"You keep him in perfect peace whose mind is stayed on You, because he trusts in You" (Isaiah 26:3).

From what I understand, when flying a plane it's possible to become so disoriented you don't know if you are upside down or right side up. In flying through fog, into a storm, or in whiteout conditions, it's easy for a pilot to become extremely disoriented. And when they lose their sense of direction, poor decision making is unfortunately just around the bend. So, what's a pilot to do? They must make the conscious choice to believe their instrument panel rather than what their eyes and instincts are screaming at them to do next. In difficult situations, the successful pilot has learned to trust the far more reliable instruments than their own subjective feelings.

When we are perplexed with life believing God doesn't care or has made a huge mistake, the instrument panel of God's Word speaks to us what is true. Perhaps it's a financial setback, the betrayal of a friend, living single in a married world, a diagnosis, or the death of a loved one far too young. These are the storms of life that disorient us. If we choose to ignore the instrument panel God has given us, we do so at our own peril, for this will only foster our natural inclinations toward confusion, disappointment, and anger. Here then is the hard work of Isaiah 26:3: Keeping our minds "stayed" on the Lord, trusting Him and the Bible in ways we cannot see or understand, in places where we must learn to be content with mystery.

The Prince of Peace

"Peace I leave with you, My peace I give to you;
not as the world gives do I give to you.
Let not your heart be troubled, neither let it be afraid"
(John 14:27).

We all want peace. Who doesn't want world peace? Closer to home, we want peace in our family relationships. Peace with co-workers, friends, and neighbors. And sometimes we just want some peace and quiet. But in the end, what we all truly want is inner peace. Peace with the past, peace for the present, and peace about the future. So maybe let's start there. How do we begin to experience this inner peace Jesus was talking about in John 14:27? To have this peace *of* God, you must first have peace *with* God. *"Therefore, having been justified by faith, we have peace with God through our Lord Jesus Christ"* (Romans 5:1). A few verses later, Paul says, *"For if when we were enemies we were reconciled to God through the death of His Son..."* (v. 10). Without reconciliation, enemies will remain enemies. And left in that state, there will never be any peace between enemies. This is the first step for true and lasting peace. Peace with God. For our souls, and for our world.

Once you've established peace with God, now you're able to experience the peace *of* God. The peace Jesus was talking about in John 14, and what Paul was referring to when, writing to the Philippians from a dungeon, he said,

> *"Be anxious for nothing, but in everything by prayer and supplication, with thanksgiving, let your requests be made known to God, and the peace of God, which surpasses all understanding, will guard your hearts and minds through Christ Jesus"* (Philippians 4:6-7).

That's inner peace. The gift of having peace with God. However, the paradox is you must fight for this peace. Our human ability to dwell on the past, be consumed with the present, and imagine a plethora of future scenarios doesn't comport well with inner peace. But it's there, He says to us "trust Me", and He calls us to *"Be still, and know that I am God"* (Psalm 46:10).

Living in this Day and Age

"If we are going to be destroyed by an atomic bomb, let that bomb when it comes find us doing sensible and human things—praying, working, teaching, reading, listening to music, bathing the children, playing tennis, chatting to our friends over a pint and a game of darts—not huddled together like frightened sheep and thinking about bombs. They might break our bodies (a microbe can do that) but they need not dominate our minds." C.S. Lewis

"So do not fear, for I am with you; do not be dismayed, for I am your God. I will strengthen you and help you; I will uphold you with my righteous right hand" (Isaiah 41:10).

It doesn't take much to remind us things are pretty much the same since C. S. Lewis wrote this back in 1948. At the time of this writing, the ongoing war in Ukraine has for months threatened to escalate to the nuclear level, and now more recently Israel has gone to war. The specter of a nuclear holocaust continues to loom over us these seventy-five years later.

So, what are we to do? Simply put, God wants us to come to Him. Fear is real, often paralyzing, and it is powerful. But God is more powerful. When we "fear" in His presence, God will enable us to take that next step of faith. His presence, and promises made to us in the Bible, provide reassurance and give us confidence by faith. And so, what might that next step of faith look like? It may involve planting flowers, visiting someone in the hospital, or simply giving Him thanks as we enjoy His beautiful creation. Draw near to God, and He will draw near to you. Then do the next thing. (Verses putting fear in perspective: Psalm 23:4; 27:1; 46:1-3; 56:3-4; 118:6. Luke 12:7,32. John 14:27)

Returning

"Nevertheless I have this against you, that you have left your first love" (Revelation 2:4).

Like any intimate human relationship, we have here on earth, our connection with Jesus Christ is established on the basis of love (*"For God so loved the world..."* John 3:16 *"...Jesus Christ, whom having not seen you love."* 1 Peter 1:7-8 *"We love Him because He first loved us"* 1 John 4:19*)*. And like any human relationship, that love can wax and wane. Not Him to us, because *"Jesus Christ is the same yesterday, today, and forever"* (Hebrews 13:8). His unmerited love for us has no ebb and flow. Where the change occurs is in our fluctuating love for Him. Life happens, and the One who once seemed so close to us yesterday now seems so distant today. And to make matters worse, Jesus warned in our day and age lawlessness would abound, and *"the love of many will grow cold"* (Matthew 24:12)*.

So, what is the pathway to return to your first love? The parable of the sower, found in Mark chapter 4, provides three root causes that diminish our love for God:

1. *"The cares of this world"*: Busy, busy, busy, we are tyrannized by the urgent, where the sum of life digresses to merely the demands and errands of daily living. We're far too busy for God.

2. *"The deceitfulness of riches"*: It's not money that's the root of all evil. It's the *love* of money. A misguided love for money, regardless of our justification of it, will deceive us and lead us away from Him.

3. *"The desires for other things"*: In our quest to find purpose and happiness in anything and everything but God, we erroneously conclude surely, He can't be the fulfillment of such a search. And yet the psalmist says, *"Having you, I desire nothing else on earth."*

As in the story of the prodigal son, our loving Father assures us that if we return to Him, He will be there waiting to receive us with open arms.

Intertwined

"Bear with each other and forgive one another if any of you has a grievance against someone. Forgive as the Lord forgave you. And over all these virtues put on love, which binds them all together in perfect unity" (Colossians 3:13-14).

The redwoods of Northern California are truly a national wonder. Towering some 350 feet into the air, weighing over 6,000 tons, with many of them more than 2,500 years old, some of these trees are so large you can drive a truck through them. You would think to survive all the many violent storms, raging fires, and fierce winds they've encountered over the centuries these trees would possess enormous root systems extending hundreds of feet into the ground; however, that is not the case at all. In fact, the root system of a redwood is extremely shallow, going no deeper than six to ten feet underground. Then how in the world do these massive trees stand a chance of staying upright for a week, much less thousands of years?

The secret lies in their sense of community. They survive because they live in groves, with their root systems entangled and interconnected with numerous other redwoods. In other words, they stand strong because they're not standing alone. Each tree supports and protects the others. What a great picture this gives us of our need for one another. We are designed to be in a connected community, not living in isolation but having our root systems intertwined with others, providing mutual nourishment, protection, and support as we grow strong through the many and oftentimes turbulent seasons of life.

Forgiveness

"'But as for you, you meant evil against me;
but God meant it for good, in order to bring it about as it is this day,
to save many people alive. Now therefore, do not be afraid; I will
provide for you and your little ones.'
And he comforted them and spoke kindly to them"
(Genesis 50:20-21).

Long before March 17th became about leprechauns, shamrocks, pots of gold, wearing green, or Chicago coloring their river green, there was a young man by the name of Patrick. Born in 385 A.D., at the age of sixteen he was kidnapped from the Roman province of Britannia by barbarian Irish pirates. For six years he labored as an imprisoned farm hand in Northern Ireland. It was during this captivity that his previously ambivalent faith served to strengthen him during those long, dark days. Having escaped back to Britannia, he became a priest, but his love for the Irish never abated. He returned to Ireland in his mid-forties, and for the next twenty-nine years until his death on March 17, 461, built over 300 churches and baptized over 100,000 people. It was not too long ago that a New York Times' bestselling book argued that St. Patrick and his Ireland saved civilization.

Like Joseph in the book of Genesis, written thousands of years before his life, Patrick embodied the supernatural power of forgiveness. Seeing how much he had been forgiven, he in turn chose to love and lay down his life for those who sought to exploit his. Patrick wrote in his autobiography *Confessions* about his conversion while in captivity,

> "And there the Lord opened my mind to an awareness of my unbelief, in order that, even so late, I might remember my transgressions and turn with all my heart to the Lord my God, who had regard for my insignificance and pitied my youth and ignorance. And he watched over me before I knew him, and before I learned sense or even distinguished between good and evil, and he protected me, and consoled me as a father would his son."

Honoring Mothers and Fathers

*"But we were gentle among you, just as a nursing mother cherishes
her own children. So affectionately longing for you, we were well
pleased to impart to you not only the gospel of God, but also our
own lives, because you had become dear to us"
(1 Thessalonians 2:7-8).*

*"...as you know how we exhorted, and comforted, and charged every
one of you, as a father does his own children, that you would walk
worthy of God who calls you into His own kingdom and glory"
(1 Thessalonians 2:11-12).*

In late SPRING we devote entire days to honor both our mothers and our fathers. So, thanks Mom and Dad! Truly it is good to honor those people in our lives who have taken such care of us, nurtured us, and made investments into us. Speaking and showing our gratitude to them, and blessing them, is one way we reflect the love of Jesus and the kindness of the Lord to others.

No matter where or who you are in life's journey, just like parents, there is always someone younger who needs your wisdom, encouragement, input, and spiritual investment. There are many in your midst who need an older person's counsel, who could be uplifted by the love and prayers of someone who's been in their shoes. You don't need a degree or a title of "mother" or "father" to be this kind of encourager; it merely requires a willingness to invest your life in serving Him and others. But what it will require, like a mom and dad, is an intentional life. Psalm 90:12 says, *"So teach us to number our days, that we may gain a heart of wisdom."* God doesn't ask us to number our days to increase our pace, but rather to examine our course. Not to increase our efficiency, but to see where He can increase in our hearts and lives. So, thank you Mom and Dad. What may seem to you to be extremely mundane activities are to God priceless and eternal treasures.

Embracing the Brevity

"Lord, make me to know my end, and what is the measure of my days, that I may know how frail I am. Indeed, You have made my days as handbreadths, and my age is as nothing before You; certainly man at his best state is but vapor" (Psalm 39:4-5).

The SPRING calendar also recognizes Memorial Day, a time we remember and honor those who paid the ultimate sacrifice for our country. For those of us who remain and enjoy the fruit of their sacrifice, it's also a reminder of how short life really is in light of eternity. For all of us. Whether you live to eight or eighty. Consider the analogies Scripture uses for human life: a mist, vapor, a breath, a shadow, a sigh, grass that withers, and flowers that fade. But the Bible does not emphasize the brevity of life in order to minimize life's significance; on the contrary, it does so to focus our hearts on what really matters. As Moses prayed in Psalm 90, *"So teach us to number our days, that we may gain a heart of wisdom."*

And what does wisdom tell us about life? What does it say about significance, purpose, and meaning? It says to invest your life into the things offering a good return on your eternal investment, those things that will live forever. The Word of God lives forever, *"the word of God which lives and abides forever"* (1 Peter 1:23), and people live forever, *"God has given us eternal life, and this life is in His Son"* (1 John 5:11). Lives centered around and focused on that which lasts will be lives well-lived. If something as "insignificant" as a cup of cold water in Jesus' name will never be forgotten by Him, then each moment you sacrificially serve another will be a moment the Lord records with tremendous significance and purpose.

So, in the remaining fleeting time we have left here on planet earth, remember, *"God is not unjust to forget your work and labor of love which you have shown towards His name"* (Hebrews 6:10). May our temporal earthly lives produce fruit lasting forever.

The Soil of Our Hearts

"Be kind to one another, tenderhearted, forgiving one another,
as God in Christ forgave you" (Ephesians 4:32).

Come September, my May flower beds will (sadly) be a far cry from what they were at the start. The heat of SUMMER will take its toll, hardening the ground to the point where my annuals will cry out, "We give up!" and my perennials will begin asking, "When will the rains of FALL begin?" Like our Northwest soil in early fall, our hearts too can become hard from the scorching heat of hurt, betrayal, or wrongs spoken or done. As believers, we know forgiveness is necessary, and yet if we're honest, it does not come naturally or easily. What comes naturally is nursing the wound, harboring that grudge, and remembering (through endless loops of analysis) the offense done against us. We call it forgiveness when we've moved on, but I think forgiveness is when we let tenderness move in... before we've moved on.

How can we keep our hearts tender and soft? Especially when the grievance is severe, or when the offense is relatively small but close in geographical proximity... and seems to be stuck on repeat. As Christians, our ability to forgive always begins at the foot of the cross. It's there where we find the severity of our grievance and offense towards a Holy God and see the depth and degree of His forgiveness towards us. And it's there at the foot of the cross where we must keep close proximity. Each and every day. And as we do, receiving and experiencing His mercy in grateful adoration, we'll find a heart able to extend what is impossible apart from His amazing grace.

Not the Baby!

"So the king of Israel [Ahab] answered and said, 'Tell him, let not the one who puts on his armor boast like the one who takes it off'"
(1 Kings 20:11).

"There's truth in many wells," my friend said to me as we ate breakfast at the U District IHOP many years ago. While I've come to believe this deeply when it comes to truth and deepening my relationship with Jesus, at times I've also found it's quite hard, and somewhat exhausting, to sort through all the noise that emanates from all those wells. What is just noise, and what is the signal I'm to take in? Not easy when the noise is 95% and the signal is 5%. Take for instance the above quote from King Ahab of "Ahab and Jezebel" biblical infamy. Although it's been a Christian tradition over the centuries to give your children biblical names, I have yet to know of any parent who named their child Ahab or Jezebel. And yet, what he said is true. Or take King Nebuchadnezzar (know anyone by that name?), the guy who threw people into fiery furnaces. He did once utter, *"And those who walk in pride He is able to put down"* (Daniel 4:37). This too is a true statement.

We've all heard the term, "Don't throw the baby out with the bathwater." Baby good. Bathwater bad. While true that sometimes we do need to "consider the source," oftentimes this same source may think, say, or do that which should be considered. While it is far easier to judge, dismiss, and discount these sources in their entirety, God may want us to hear them and listen closely in order to gain new understanding and wisdom. So, before you dismiss the Ahabs and Nebuchadnezzars of your life, you might want to move towards them to see what truth in avoidance or rejection you might be missing.

Interruptions

"The great thing, if one can, is to stop regarding all the unpleasant things as interruptions of one's 'own', or 'real' life.
The truth is of course that what one calls the interruptions are precisely one's real life—the life God is sending one day by day: what one calls one's 'real life' is a phantom of one's own imagination."
The Letter of C. S. Lewis to Arthur Greeves

"He [Jesus] entered the synagogue and taught.
Now there was a man in their synagogue with an unclean spirit.
And he cried out....." (Mark 1:21, 23).

Wouldn't it be great to be able to hang around your neck one of those "Do Not Disturb" signs you get to put on your hotel door? Unfortunately, life's not that simple. But fortunately, as the Author (and Finisher) of our faith, God writes upon our lives unexpected twists and turns each and every day. The question is, are these a diversion from the path we should be taking, or are they in fact the path? Take for instance the life of Jesus at the beginning of the book of Mark. Thirty-five times He's interrupted in just the first three chapters. And many times, He's interrupted only to be interrupted from his interruption! *"A man's heart plans his way, but the Lord directs his steps"* (Proverbs 16:9).

So, the next time a friend calls when you are walking out the door... Or a family member drops by unannounced... Or a stranger strikes up a conversation at the airport... Or your line at the grocery store has come to a complete stop ("I need a price check on aisle three")... Remember: The Lord is in control, and He is directing your steps. Those interruptions? They actually constitute your real life. The one He is directing.

Inside Out

"Or do you show contempt for the riches of his kindness,
tolerance, and patience, not realizing that God's kindness
leads you toward repentance?" (Romans 2:4).

While God is kind, He is not soft or weak, for He's truly committed to our abandonment of sin. We are told, *"The Lord is... patient toward us, not willing that any should perish but that all should come to repentance"* (2 Peter 3:9). So together, the prior two verses teach us the role kindness and patience have in transforming us. From the inside out. What a fascinating combination of attributes the Lord employs to gain a true 180 degree *about face* in those He loves. Humans, on the other hand (insert spouses, parents, coaches, bosses, teachers, governing authorities, etc.), tend to employ more "outside in" strategies to gain what generally amounts to temporary behavioral change in others, such as coercion, manipulation, nagging, threats, yelling, or punishment.

Yes, kindness and patience changed our hearts, having been poured out upon us who had no merit in ourselves. No amount of penance, performance, or sacrifice activated these attributes in God towards us. All we brought to the table was our brokenness and sin. And what He brought was His amazing grace and love in Christ. Humbled by the infinite contrast between His holiness and our lives, we are the forever-grateful recipients of His undeserved mercy and favor. Made new by this love, we too can add these two transformative qualities into our repertoire of approaches in effecting change towards those close to us.

Have you talked to him?

"I had many things to write, but I do not wish to write to you with pen and ink; but I hope to see you shortly, and we shall speak face to face" (3 John 1:13).

At a former employer, I had a co-worker who was very difficult to work with. Since he and I both reported to the same person, at best I would go meet with her and whine and complain about him, or at worst I would just shoot off a fiery email to her grumbling about the latest dumb (so I thought) thing he had done or said. Always, her first response was to ask, "Have you talked to him?" And of course, my answer was always a sheepish "no." She always directed me to the thing I did not want to do but needed to do. She directed me, and also coached me, to have crucial conversations.

Crucial conversations are when the stakes are high, opinions vary, and emotions run strong. That kind of conversation is really hard when the norm for our region is "Seattle Nice." We tend to be a more passive aggressive sort here in the northwest. Prone to hide behind the façade we're all just "fine," a cold war can quickly brew because of the core value so many of us share of outward niceness. To make matters worse, it's much easier to hide behind our technology and fire off the latest text or email tirade to those we disagree or are angry with. And of course, digitally going dark and ghosting are even easier ways to avoid the conflict we so dread.

A pastor once said, "Never say no because of fear." Rather than firing off that email, go do the hard thing. Talk to the person. God has given us the ministry of reconciliation, and that almost always occurs face to face.

Water Off a Duck's Back

"This was to show God's righteousness, because in His divine forbearance he had passed over former sins" (Romans 3:25).

Forbearance is not a word you hear much these days. While I've lost count the number of times forgiveness came into play, I can't recall a single time where those involved cried out for greater forbearance. What does it even mean to forbear? The word means to patiently restrain an impulse to do something, to refrain; to be long-suffering, willing to put up with people's actions and inactions—to let things go. In essence, forbearance is a by-product of love, the kind of love Paul expressed in 1 Corinthians 13, a love that *"is not provoked....does not take into account a wrong suffered... .bears all things, believes all things, hopes all things, endures all things."*

A lack of forbearance in our homes and in the workplace exaggerates offenses, magnifies tension, and intensifies conflict. It erects walls in relationships, makes us petty, and severs relationships. It comes from the little things we allow to get under our skin from those who are frequently in close proximity to us. This is the truth behind the idiom *"familiarity breeds contempt."* On the other hand, practicing the grace of forbearance and letting the little things go is a form of love. Yes, bigger issues will arise, requiring a great measure of forgiveness. Learning to forbear today is a valuable practice for being able to forgive later.

Perfectly Joined Together

"For as we have many members in one body, but all the members do not have the same function, so we, being many, are one body in Christ, and individually members of one another" (Romans 12:4-5).

Living in a world with so much angry strife, extreme polarization, and lonely disconnection, imagine a world where trust and love bind us together. Where people assume the best of intentions in other people, where others are innocent until proven otherwise, where people serve others and bear their burdens, where the interests of others are regarded more highly than our own. Wouldn't that be a great place to be? Marjie and I share a similar aspiration to explore what this might look like this side of heaven. Sadly, it's hard to find many positive examples here on earth, but fortunately God gave us a very tangible one—our human body. Do you know you have ten different systems (and many sub-systems) in your body? Digestive, cardiovascular, respiratory, lymphatic, nervous, to name a few. Nervous can't do digestive, and respiratory would fail in doing cardiovascular's job. But to say they rigidly stay in their own swim lanes would be inaccurate, because they're all organically intertwined.

And so is the body of Christ. Each part doing what they do best, but each part organically connected to the others. We're not books on a shelf, where one can be pulled out and it doesn't impact the others. Or marbles in a bag, where we're just bouncing off one another while in close proximity. No, my finger can only be at its best when connected to my body. Apart from my body, it can do nothing. I believe this way of thinking was also Paul's, for he wrote *"...that there be no divisions among you, but that you be perfectly joined together..."* (1 Corinthians 1:10). Maybe we'll never fully experience what it is in perfection, but let's aspire to it, for Jesus said, *"They'll know you are my disciples because of the love you have for one another"* (John 13:35).

Need a Good Nickname?

"Joseph, a Levite from Cyprus, whom the apostles called Barnabas (which means "son of encouragement"), sold a field he owned and brought the money and put it at the apostles' feet" (Acts 4:36-37).

Reading through the book of Acts, you would be hard pressed to remember anyone by the name of Joseph. But Barnabas? Now that's a name that keeps popping up. It seems the apostles liked to pass around nicknames based on character qualities, and Joseph was no exception. Here are five attributes of his life that jump out to us from the book of Acts:

1. **He was generous** (*see 4:37 above*): You may not have a field to sell, but giving back what God has given you serves to encourage and comfort those around us. You can't outgive God!

2. **He built bridges between people when others preferred walls** (*"And when Saul.....tried to join the disciples....they were afraid of him and did not believe he was a disciple...But Barnabas took him and brought him to the disciples" Acts 9:26-27):* We encourage others when we befriend and love the marginalized, inviting those on the outside in.

3. **He valued relationships and spoke words of life in building others up** (*"...they sent out Barnabas to go as far as Antioch. When he came and had seen the grace of God, he was glad, and encouraged them all with purpose of heart they should continue with the Lord" Acts 11:22-23):* It's easy to tear others down and see the negative, but Barnabas was always seeking ways to build others up with his words.

4. **He saw the potential in others and sought their growth and development** (*"Then Barnabas departed for Tarsus to seek Saul. And when he had found him, he brought him to Antioch" Acts 11:25-26):* And for the next year, Paul would teach alongside Barnabas in Antioch, growing and developing into the one who would someday write the bulk of the New Testament.

5. **He remained with those others had rejected** (*"Now Barnabas was determined to take with them Mark. But Paul insisted that they should not take with them the one who had departed from them. So Barnabas took Mark and sailed for Cyprus" Acts 15:37-39.):* Mark would go on to reconcile with Paul and write the Gospel of Mark, but it was the encouraging loyalty of Barnabas that saw him through this low point of discouragement and rejection.

What began as a nickname ended as an appropriate epitaph of a life well-lived.

SUMMER

To plant a garden is to believe in tomorrow.
Audrey Hepburn

Fruitfulness

As Steve mentioned earlier, SUMMER is my most favorite season. The reasons for this are plentiful! For one, I love the warm weather. I was raised in the desert southwest, so I much prefer warmth rather than cold. Now I live in the Pacific Northwest, and summertime provides lush green hills, mountains, yards, flowers, abundant garden containers, and bountiful blooming beauty everywhere the eye can see.

As a mom of four, I came to appreciate the SUMMERS, because all of our school schedules came to a screeching halt! My children were off for three months, and this provided us time as a family to enjoy a more relaxed pace, get outside together, and create great vacation memories.

SUMMER is also a season when Steve and I mark our wedding anniversary. June 27 has become one of our most favorite dates on the calendar!

As a Bible teacher, I have historically used the SUMMER months to reset and refresh. This is the season where I plan and write out the next session of the Bible study that I am a part of. This process has become one that requires many hours of my time, so SUMMERTIME for me is also a season of growth, stretching, labor, and intention.

My life verse is John 15:8: *"This is my Father's glory that you bear much fruit, showing yourselves to be my disciples."* This verse has truly guided my decisions as an adult, and especially when it comes to how I invest my time. While SUMMERS for many are filled with vacations and rest, mine are sometimes filled with a good amount of labor. This verse reminds me of my purpose and ultimately, my hope.

I spend a great deal of my SUMMERS studying and writing, but my goal is to glorify God and to bear much fruit for Him. If I can help instill hope and encouragement in others through the study of His Word, then I am living out my purpose.

SUMMERS are filled with goodness and growth, and especially the kind that bears fruit for our good King!

God's Promises to You

"His divine power has given us everything we need for life and godliness through our knowledge of Him who called us by His own glory and goodness. Through these He has given us His very great and precious promises, so that through them you may participate in the divine nature and escape the corruption in the world caused by evil desires" (2 Peter 1:3-4).

The SUMMERS of life are very demanding. When you are in the battle, every day will bring some new opposition or adversity to face. As we seek to expand His kingdom here on earth, any thrust we attempt against the gates of hell will be met with commensurate resistance and hostility. That's just life. And so, when you are in the thick of the battle, it can be very discouraging at times. Weariness is constantly crouching at the door, and fatigue becomes the new normal. But this is where the living and active Word of God becomes our offensive weapon to fight and defeat the enemy of our souls. Like Jesus when He began His earthly ministry, we too must rely upon the powerful Word of God to win our assigned battles. The promises of God not only enable us to survive the winds and waves of life—they also equip us to thrive in victory over all this world and the devil can throw at us.

The Lord's divine power, coupled with His very great and precious promises, enable and equip us with everything we need for life and godliness. Everything! Everything we need for all of life can be found in these promises...now that's encouraging! And this is why *"we do not live on bread alone, but on every Word that proceeds from the mouth of God"* (Matthew 4:4).

Your Presence is My Confidence

"For all the promises of God in Christ are Yes, and in Him Amen, to the glory of God through us" (2 Corinthians 1:20).

One incredible outcome of the finished work of Jesus Christ is every promise in the Bible is now applicable for you today. So, when God made a promise to Joshua way back in the Old Testament, that promise is now true and applicable for you to take hold of. Back then, Joshua was told to go take the promised land, and everywhere he set his foot it was his (Joshua 1:2-3). But he needed two things to carry this out. Three times he is told to be strong and courageous. But how? There were giants in the land! The answer is found in Joshua 1:9:

> *"Have I not commanded you? Be strong and of good courage; do not be afraid, nor be dismayed, for the Lord your God is with you wherever you go."*

This day as you go about your assignments, remember the Lord is with you. God's word to Joshua then is God's word to you now: *"Be strong and of good courage."* The earth is your promised land, and everywhere you set your foot, it's been given to you. The presence of Christ makes you strong and courageous, able to face any obstacle or opposition that may come your way. For He has also said, *"All authority has been given to Me in heaven and on earth, therefore go......and lo, I am with you always, even to the end of the age"* (Matthew 28:18-20).

Not Losing Heart

*"Let us not become weary in doing good, for at the proper time
we will reap a harvest if we do not give up (or lose heart)"
(Galatians 6:9).*

I love this promise. We *will* reap. But what might limit us from seeing that harvest? Losing heart. Getting weary and giving up. We all feel it at times. This is why I believe the #1 tool the enemy uses is discouragement. It's his "gateway drug" of choice, the first step he employs to ultimately circumvent us from ever reaching that harvest we were designed by God to reap.

And here's another promise I read repeatedly when I want to throw in the towel: *"I would have lost heart, unless I had believed that I would see the goodness of the Lord in the land of the living"* (Psalm 27:13). That's right: I *am* going to see the goodness of the Lord in the land of living. I'm not dead yet. I'm still in the land of the living, and so I am going to see the goodness of the Lord in my life right here on earth.

Why? Because He promises *"surely goodness and mercy will follow me all the days of my life"* (Psalm 23:6).

We are called "believers" for a reason. Let's take God at His Word and believe what He says is true and applies to all the many details (both great and small) of our lives.

Welcoming Resistance

*"Do you not know that in a race all the runners run, but only one
gets the prize? Run in such a way as to get the prize.
Everyone who competes in the games goes into strict training.
They do it to get a crown that will not last, but we do it to get
a crown that will last forever" (1 Corinthians 9:24-25).*

There are many clear and evident correlations between the physical and spiritual realms in which we live. In the physical realm, anyone who has ever worked out knows what it is like to face resistance. Weightlifters must press against resistance in order to increase their power. They will intentionally look for certain equipment to isolate a muscle they have targeted for growth. They are eager to press against this opposition to achieve their goal of increased strength in that specific area. This level of athlete is willing to suffer through intense, demanding training and embrace that which is both difficult and challenging because they have a greater objective in mind.

In the same way, each day we are faced with spiritual opposition and resistance. When faced with such problems, these are our opportunities to grow and increase our "load-bearing capacity", giving us greater strength today as God prepares us for our future. Wise believers target areas of growth now, and intentionally press against resistance in these areas. When faced with daily adversity coming from people or life's circumstances, these areas may include joy, hope, faith, gratitude, forgiveness, love, or generosity. Fortunately, God has equipped us to grow these spiritual muscles of ours by His grace and His *"exceedingly great and precious promises"* (2 Peter 1:4). As we trust the Lord and believe these promises despite opposition to the contrary, we'll end up finding ourselves *"strong in the Lord and in the power of His might"* (Ephesians 6:10).

Need a Lifeline?

*"For we do not have a High Priest who cannot sympathize with
our weaknesses, but was in all points tempted as we are,
yet without sin. Let us therefore come boldly to the throne of grace,
that we may obtain mercy and find grace to help in time of need"
(Hebrews 4:15-16).*

I (Steve... Marjie is a good swimmer) am a horrible swimmer. On more than one occasion, I have been on the brink of going under. Thus, over the years, I've become quite the expert when it comes to the type of person you want coming to your rescue. There are basically two qualities you want to have in this kind of person. First, you want them to be highly competent in their ability to swim. And second, you want them to be sympathetic to your plight. A good swimmer who just watches you drown is of no help, and a bad swimmer trying to help isn't going to be of much use either.

When Jesus was physically on the earth, He never sinned. He was tempted to do so, but in the end, He never did. So now that He is exalted to the right hand of His Father, what feeling towards us does He now possess? Sympathy. No condemnation or judgement. He doesn't accuse us of being horrible swimmers. And what's more, that sympathy always converts into mercy and grace to help in our time of need. Not 50% of the time. Or even 90% of the time. But 100% of the time, when we feel like we are about to drown, we can boldly go to the throne of grace and get the help we need.

So, is today a time of need for you? Then go to Him. In doing so you are promised to receive both mercy and grace. Just like Peter when he came face to face with his drowning experience:

"He [Peter] walked on the water to go to Jesus, but when he saw the wind was boisterous, he was afraid; and beginning to sink he cried out, saying "Lord, save me!". And immediately Jesus stretched out His hand and caught him" (Matthew 14:29-31).

Soul Food

"In the day when I cried out, You answered me,
and made me bold with strength in my soul"
(Psalm 138:3).

We all experience dark nights of the soul. Times of trouble, struggle, and weariness. In these times, it is very tempting to reply, "fine" when asked how we're doing, regardless of the storm occurring behind the scenes. We're probably hesitant to speak the honest truth to others for a myriad of reasons, but I imagine we most often suspect the other person really just doesn't care. The encouragement I find in the above verse is the Lord always does. Four facts are found here:

1. God is always there for you *"In the day when I cried out..."* Not tomorrow. You just need to seek Him.

2. God answers prayers. *"You answered me."* It may not be as you think it should, but He will.

3. God makes you courageous *"and made me bold". Courage* to face anything. Today. In the moment. And not that God made the "thing" go away. It's still there.

4. God fortifies your soul *"with strength in my soul."* Regardless of the storm you may be in, your soul can always find strength from and in Him.

From the hymn *Turn Your Eyes Upon Jesus:*

"O soul are you weary and troubled?
No light in the darkness you see?
There's light for a look at the Savior,
and life more abundant and free!

Turn your eyes upon Jesus,
look full in His wonderful face,
and the things of earth will grow strangely dim
in the light of His glory and grace."

Strength for Today

"As your days, so shall your strength be" (Deuteronomy 33:25).

We all have good days and bad days. Some days are filled with joy and laughter, while others are dark and perplexing. And all of us have had extremely bad hair days. Regardless of the day you might be facing today, you have a promise from God. If you are a Christian, and if you are alive, then today you have a strength not your own to face it. Whether your day brings you joy or brings you trial, it will not matter. God has promised to send you exactly the strength you need to pass through it victoriously.

A favorite hymn of mine is *Day by Day:*

> *Day by day and with each passing moment,*
> *strength I find to meet my trials here;*
> *trusting in my Father's wise bestowment,*
> *I've no cause for worry or for fear.*

> *He whose heart is kind beyond all measure*
> *gives unto each day what He deems best,*
> *lovingly it's part of pain and pleasure,*
> *mingling toil with peace and rest.*

> *Every day the Lord Himself is near me*
> *with a special mercy for each hour;*
> *all my cares He fain would bear and cheer me,*
> *He whose name is Counselor and Power.*

> *The protection of His child and treasure*
> *is a charge that on Himself he laid;*
> *"As your days, your strength shall be in measure,"*
> *this the pledge to me He made.*

Slip Sliding Away

*"Therefore, we must give the more earnest heed to the things
we have heard, lest we drift away" (Hebrews 2:1).*

Drifting away from something or someone, while it may be quite literally imperceptible as it's happening, may frequently have an end diametrically opposed to its beginning. Unbeknownst to those onboard, a boat not securely anchored at night can find itself miles from shore in the morning. Couples once so intimately close, drift apart and permanently separate in divorce. Groups and organizations form a mission statement, but as the years go by, mission drift sets in and the end is the antithesis of the start. For instance, established by the Puritans in 1636 with a mission to train clergy for the new commonwealth, Harvard recently hired an atheist as their Chief Chaplain.

What steps can we take to ensure we don't drift away in our relationship with the Lord? Fortunately, the book of Hebrews was written to answer this very question. Three times over the course of just nineteen verses the writer tells us,

"Today, if you will hear His voice, do not harden your hearts as in the rebellion" (Hebrews 3:7-8, 15; 4:7). Led by Moses out of Egypt, the people rebelled and wandered forty years in the desert, possessing *"an evil heart of unbelief in departing from the living God"* (3:12).

When we, on the other hand, hear God's voice *today* (not yesterday or tomorrow) as He speaks to us from His Word, and we *"mix it with faith"* (4:2), this is how *"we hold the beginning of our confidence steadfast to the end"* (3:14).

Why is that? Because when we read and believe, *"the word of God is living and powerful"* (4:12). Therefore, the writer encourages us to *"come boldly to the throne of grace, that we may obtain* mercy *and find grace to help in time of need"* (4:16).

So today, *"Draw near to God, and He will draw near to you"* (James 4:8).

Victors

"Now thanks be to God who always leads us in triumph in Christ, and through us diffuses the fragrance of His knowledge in every place"
(2 Corinthians 2:14).

Paul is alluding to one of the most spectacular and important celebrations in antiquity, the Roman Triumph. The Triumph was essentially an enormous parade through the heart of Rome honoring a victorious general and his victory over yet another Roman enemy. The city would be adorned to embrace her conquering hero, with incense rising from every temple in the city. The paradox of Paul's allusion is how this victory is achieved in the Christian life. While we know Christ is that conquering general, like Him the triumphant life of the believer cannot be defined by earthly standards.

Later in this letter, Paul goes on to say how he has been hard-pressed, perplexed, persecuted, fearful, downcast, weary, sleepless, and struck down. Flogged five times, three times beaten with rods, three times shipwrecked, and once stoned, Paul by any definition was not triumphant by outward appearances. And yet he knew in Christ he was always victorious, for he walked by faith and not by sight. For later he states,

"Now we have this treasure in earthen vessels, that the excellence of the power may be of God and not of us. Therefore, we do not lose heart. Even though our outward man is perishing, yet the inward man is being renewed day by day. For our light affliction, which is but for a moment, is working for us a far more exceeding and eternal weight of glory, while we do not look at the things which are seen, but at the things that are not seen" (2 Corinthians 4:7; 16-18).

Like Paul, the victorious life comes when you embrace your frailties, for then His *"grace is sufficient for you, for My strength is made perfect in weakness"* (2 Corinthians 12:9).

The Reality Behind Reality

"Finally, be strong in the Lord and in his mighty power.
Put on the full armor of God, so that you can take your
stand against the devil's schemes.
For our struggle is not against flesh and blood,
but against rulers, against the authorities, against the powers
of this dark world and against the spiritual forces of evil in the
heavenly realms. Therefore put on the full armor of God,
so that when the day of evil comes, you may be able to stand your
ground, and after you have done everything, to stand"
(Ephesians 6:10-13).

What we call the real world is indeed real, in that it is discerned by our five senses: we can see, touch, hear, smell, and/or taste it. But the Bible speaks of truth, for Jesus said, *"I am the truth"* (John 14:6), and *"the truth will set you free"* (John 8:32). And so, we need to have a mindset of making God's truth primary in our lives, always superseding, and bringing perspective to our reality. Trusting in Truth is called *faith*. The above passage tells us the truth about the difficult people in our lives. Adversarial relationships… people with names… are not the problem. Who we are really struggling with is actually unseen. This is why we can supernaturally love our enemies, because fundamentally they are not the problem. This is why, as He hung dying on the cross, Jesus could say, *"Father forgive them, for they know not what they do"* (Luke 23:34).

This week we all will have difficult people, situations, and conversations to face. Keep in the forefront of your mind, your struggle is not against (insert name here). Knowing the true source of our struggle with others will free us up to *"love your enemies, bless those who curse you, do good to those who hate you, and pray for those who spitefully use you and persecute you"* (Matthew 5:44).

For the truth will set us free.

The Deep End

"And Moses said to Joshua,
'Choose us some men and go out, fight with Amalek'"
(Exodus 17:9).

Have you ever been pushed into the deep end of a pool before you really knew how to swim? It's quite frightening not having the safety net of your toes touching the bottom. I think we've all found the same principle true in the pool of life. Oftentimes we find ourselves pushed into something, and we feel like we're about to drown. Take Joshua for example. The above verse is the first time he's ever mentioned in the Bible. There's no evidence he attended a military academy, went to boot camp, or had practice drills. No courses in war strategy or even experience as soldier. And to top it off, for his very first time in battle, he's commissioned to be the general. Good luck with that. Forget victory, will he even survive? (BTW: By the grace of God, Joshua was victorious.)

Maybe you're in a situation similar to Joshua's. Thrown into a battle with no prior experience or preparation. Learning on the job, you're having to navigate challenging family dynamics, a medical diagnosis, legal issues, financial pressures, work conundrums, or a broken friendship in need of reconciliation. Blindsided, you see no conceivable way to make it through what God has placed upon you. But maybe that's the point. By design, maybe God is putting you in that very position where sinking or defeat is a legitimate possibility. Just like Peter when he began to sink into the water but *"cried out, 'Lord save me!'"* (Matthew 14:30). And Jesus did. Do you want to see God work powerfully in your life? Then stay in the battle and watch how your desperation and inadequacy will provide the perfect setting to experience Him working through you.

Strong and Active Influencers

*"The people who know their God will be strong and take action.
Those who have insight among the people will give understanding to
many" (Daniel 11:32-33).*

The Hebrew verb translated "have insight" in this passage is *sakal*. It can mean "to be wise," "to understand," to "have skill," or to "have insight." It refers to the wisdom, skill, and understanding everyone wants but only God's people can have. *Sakal* makes us different. It makes our faith unmistakable. We see this later in the book of Daniel when the angel says to him,

> *"Those who have insight* [sakal] *will shine like the bright expanse of the heavens, and those who lead many to righteousness, like the stars forever and ever"* (Daniel 12:3).

You are that *sakal* person. Your God-given wisdom, understanding, and skill, coupled with your humble, prayerful demeanor, makes you a bright light that stands out as the stars do on the darkest of nights. Your life makes a difference. *Sakal* men and women always do. Like Daniel, *sakal* people don't necessarily have easy lives, but they do bring light and blessing to all around them. Even with enemy forces attempting to thwart us, and the steady rain of conflict falling down upon our heads, we are not paralyzed in the process. Instead, the Lord empowers us with His courage and strength, reflecting His light in a dark world as we simply *"take action"* each and every day.

Fear Not

"Fear not, for I am with you; be not dismayed, for I am your God. I will strengthen you, yes, I will help you, I will uphold you with My righteous right hand. For I, the Lord your God, will hold your right hand, saying to you, 'Fear not, I will help you'" (Isaiah 41:10, 13).

Our world appears to be coming apart at the seams. And at times our lives can feel the same way. Thank God for His promises, which He provides to reassure us, to build up our strength, and to leave us with hope.

Fear not, for I am with you:
Never will He leave us or forsake us.

Be not dismayed, for I am your God:
Dismayed is another word for distress, which is a response we feel when something sudden or unexpected happens to us. When life blindsides us, we can be reassured He never will be.

I will strengthen you, yes, I will help you:
When you feel like you can't go on, He promises to be there to ensure you do.

I will uphold you with My righteous right hand:
When you lose your footing, He will be there to hold you up and keep you from falling.

Fear not, I will help you:
As it says in Proverbs, *"the righteous are as bold as a lion."* His presence is our confidence.

But the Lord

"But the Lord stood with me and strengthened me..."
(2 Timothy 4:17).

Paul wrote his second letter to Timothy from a dark and damp Roman prison cell, just before his execution in AD 67 during the reign of the evil Roman Emperor Nero. Chronologically, it is the last of his thirteen letters found in the Bible. And so, at the very end of this very last letter he would ever write, Paul openly shares about his broken and severed relationships as he pens his final words. For like Jesus, in the end for Paul there was only abandonment, opposition, and betrayal from all those around him. Paul closes his letter by sharing how all have deserted or opposed him: *"Demas has forsaken me" (v 10), "Alexander the coppersmith did me much harm" (v 14),* and finally *"At my first defense no one stood with me, but all forsook me" (v 16).* Utterly forsaken as he sits in solitary confinement, Paul has been rejected by his enemies and abandoned by those closest to him.

Live long enough, and you too will experience trials, grief, and hardships that will try your soul. Friends will abandon and betray you. Loved ones will suffer pain, and you will deeply grieve the loss of those closest to you. In addition, you will face opposition in both circumstantial and human forms. And if by some miracle you escape all this, in the very passing from this life to the next, you will do so alone with no human companion. So now, let's draw near to the One who is already near to us, the One who will never leave us or forsake us. For *"God is our refuge and strength, an ever-present help in times of trouble"* (Psalm 46:1). He will faithfully stand with you and give you the resilient strength you need to face all that will come your way. For He is that *"friend who sticks closer than a brother"* (Proverbs 18:24), so that you *"can do all things through Christ who strengthens you"* (Philippians 4:13). And at the end of your days, you too will be able to declare of your life, *"But the Lord stood with me and strengthened me."*

That Sinking Feeling

"And Peter answered Him and said, "Lord, if it is You, command me to come to You on the water. So He said, "Come." And when Peter had come down out of the boat, he walked on the water to go to Jesus. But when he saw the wind, he was afraid; and beginning to sink, he cried out, saying, "Lord, save me!" (Matthew 14:28-30).

Which Peter can you most relate to—the one who walked on water, or the one who began to sink? If I'm honest, I tend to relate much more with the latter. Even though Scripture tells us to *"approach God with confidence"* (Hebrews 4:16) and to *"come to God with boldness"* (Ephesians 3:12), I find when I gaze upon the winds and waves of life, my confidence and boldness begin to sink. Taking my eyes off Jesus and gazing onto the myriad of problems we all experience (too much to do and not enough time, financial insecurity, rocky relationships, growing cultural darkness, etc. etc.), it's easy to begin sinking beneath the weight of life.

But here's the good news—Peter did not sink. Even though I'm sure he felt like he was about to die, he in fact did not. He stayed afloat. How? He cried out to the Lord. *"...and beginning to sink he cried out, saying 'Lord, save me!'"*

What's giving you a sinking feeling today? What threatens to overwhelm your confidence in Jesus? Don't tread water, and don't sink into despair. Cry out to the Lord. And discover, like Peter, that His hand is already extended toward you. *"And immediately Jesus stretched out His hand and caught him..."* (v. 31).

Too Much to Handle

*"We were burdened beyond measure, above strength,
so that we despaired even of life" (2 Corinthians 1:8).*

I recently heard a color commentator say, "God will not give you more than you can handle." He did not reference a source, but it definitely was not from the Bible. Like other common phrases not found in the Bible (Money is the root of all evil. Cleanliness is next to godliness. God helps those who help themselves.), this particular phrase is actually contrary to what the Bible teaches. As the above verse suggests, the very person who wrote the bulk of the New Testament experienced burdens beyond his ability to comprehend, forces that showed how feeble and frail he was, and a despair especially reserved for those who have been handed a sentence of death. In essence, he was like you and I—he had much more than he could handle.

Now why does God do that? Fortunately, Paul goes on to give us the answer. He brings us to the very end of our rope so *"that we should not trust in ourselves but in God who raises the dead"* (v. 9). Unfortunately, as humans we like to exhaust all our efforts before turning to God. We desperately pray with two outs in the bottom of the ninth inning in the seventh game of the World Series. But in the first inning of the first game of the season? No Lord, we got this.

So repeatedly throughout life, God keeps drawing us back to Him with situations, people, and circumstances beyond our ability to handle.

But here's the good news—we can trust Him for the entirety of our lives. From beginning to end. Good times and bad times. As Paul concluded, *"...we should not trust in ourselves but in God who raises the dead, who delivered us from so great a death, and does deliver us; in whom we trust that He will still deliver us"* (v. 10). His ever-present help will enable you to handle your past, present, and future.

How to be Earthly Good

"If then you were raised with Christ, seek those things which are above, where Christ is, sitting at the right hand of God. Set your mind on things above, not on things on the earth. For you died, and your life is hidden with Christ in God. When Christ who is our life appears, then you also will appear with Him in glory"
(Colossians 3:1-4).

There was a contemporary Christian song in my younger days warning "if we are too heavenly-minded we'll be no earthly good." While I understand the sentiment of these lyrics, the Bible indicates a clear need for us to be just that—heavenly-minded. For with this as our mindset, Paul then spends the rest of the letter to the Colossians telling them how to be earthly good— displaying mercy, kindness, forgiveness, saying thank you, putting away swearing, anger, coveting, while giving specific direction to wives, husbands, children, employers, and employees. All very tangible stuff.

With a true and living *"hope that is stored up for you in heaven"* (Colossians 1:5), this then is our motivating force of joy here on earth. We who have this hope in us can go about our daily labors with renewable energy, for the *"joy of the Lord is our strength"* (Nehemiah 8:10). Life on earth is full of adversity, daily being tempted internally and opposed externally, but we persevere by grace for we long to hear those words that await us on the other side, *"Well done, good and faithful servant... enter into the joy of your Lord"* (Matthew 25:23).

Cracked Pots

"But we have this treasure in jars of clay, to show that the surpassing power belongs to God and not to us"
(2 Corinthians 4:7).

Clay pots may look sturdy and strong on the outside, but in reality, they're very fragile and quite easy to chip or break. And because they're so porous, they absorb moisture like a sponge and are prone to crack as the clay expands and contracts with the weather. What an accurate metaphor for the human condition. God's plan from the beginning was to take broken, cracked, and imperfect people like you and me and do something extraordinary. And yet, there are times when the weight of life feels so great, we are sure our own personal jar of clay will soon be crushed under the load.

But God has given us a gift. A treasure. He's given Himself. Living inside us, the Holy Spirit enables these fragile clay jars to somehow walk in victory. *"Hard-pressed on every side, yet not crushed"* (2 Cor. 4:8). *"Now thanks be to God who always leads us in triumph in Christ, and through us diffuses the fragrance of His knowledge in every place"* (2 Cor. 2:14). To the point where Paul could conclude,

> *"Therefore we do not lose heart. Even though our outward man is perishing, yet the inward man is being renewed day by day. For our light affliction, which is but for a moment, is working for us a far more exceeding and eternal weight of glory"* (2 Cor. 4:16-17).

And so, *"If God is for you, who can be against you?"* In all the many trials and tribulations of life, *"...we are more than conquerors through Him who loved us"* (Romans 8:31, 37).

Ambitious for the Hidden Life

"Make it your ambition to lead a quiet life, to mind your own business, and to work with your own hands..."
(1 Thessalonians 4:11).

Don't we all, to some degree, desire significance and to make a difference in the world? How to achieve it is the big question. Many voices in our world tell us to be ambitious for fame and fortune, thinking that is how important and lasting change will truly be achieved. While bright lights might glitter for some, most of us choose not to chase these shiny objects. So, what then? How do we fulfill this hunger for purpose and to make a difference in this brief time we have down here? Christ both showed and told us how. He showed us by touching the leper, by seeking the woman at the well, and by healing the man born blind. He told us about the shepherd leaving the ninety-nine to find the one, about visiting the solitary prisoner, housing the lonely stranger, and giving food to the one who is hungry. *"Assuredly, I say to you, inasmuch as you did it to one of the least of these, you did it to Me"* (Matthew 25:40). To God, it's always about the one.

George Eliot, an English novelist from the 1800's, wrote:

> "...for the growing good of the world is partly dependent on unhistoric acts; and that things are not so ill with you and me as they might have been, is half owing to the number who lived faithfully a hidden life and rest in unvisited tombs."

Strength to Strength

*"But you, be strong and do not let your hands be weak,
for your work shall be rewarded!" (2 Chronicles 15:7).*

Immediately after hearing these words from the prophet, Asa the King of Judah *"took courage"* (v. 8). Hearing that God saw him and would reward his work gave Asa the strength he needed for the task at hand. What's true for Asa is true for you and me. Every promise in Christ Jesus our Lord is *"Yes and Amen"* (2 Corinthians 1:20), so this promise to Asa is now applicable for us in Christ. God sees you; He says be strong, and that your work will be rewarded. So have courage this day as you receive His divine strength.

Psalm 84:7 also says *"we go from strength to strength."* Meaning, as we take courage and exhibit strength, we become stronger. By grace, what once overcame us, we now overcome. *"For whoever has, to him more will be given, and he will have in abundance"* (Matthew 13:12). Asa was later reminded of this principle of increasing strength in 2 Chronicles 16:9:

> *"For the eyes of the Lord run to and fro throughout the whole earth, to show Himself strong on behalf of those whose heart is loyal to Him."*

Do you want to be strong? Look to Him, for He is still looking to strengthen those whose hearts trust in Him.

Praying the Names of God

"The name of the Lord is a strong tower.
The righteous run into it and are safe" (Proverbs 18:10).

In Hebrew and Greek, a personal name communicated something crucial for distinguishing a person's character and personality. In the Bible, when God would reveal Himself to someone, He often used His name. He did this after people experienced Him in a deep way in response to their immediate need. For instance, when God provided a ram to sacrifice rather than his son Isaac, Abraham called Him *"Jehovah-Jireh"* (The Lord Will Provide). When Hagar was alone, feeling invisible, and that no one cared, God saw and cared for her, so she called him *"El Roi"* (The God Who Sees). And when the people of Israel were tempted to fear disease, God said to them He was *"Jehovah-Rapha"* (The Lord Who Heals).

For every situation you are facing today, there is a name or attribute of God corresponding to that immediate need. When we pray and focus on who God says He is, we orient ourselves toward the One who has the jurisdiction, authority, power, and desire to intervene in our lives. He is: Abba Father (Abba is a Greek word describing a close, intimate relationship between a father and child), Comforter, Deliverer, Father of Mercy, Never-Failing One, Quieting Love, Very Present Help, The Lifter of your head. And so many more.

When we pray the names of God, we are doing what Jesus modeled when He said, *"This, then, is how you should pray: 'Our Father, who art in Heaven, hallowed be your name'"* (Matthew 6:9). And like David, we too can say, *"Oh magnify the Lord with me, and let us exalt His name together"* (Psalm 34:3).

Do The Next Thing

"A man's heart plans his way,
but the Lord directs his steps" (Proverbs 16:9).

In the 1950's, the missionary couple Jim and Elisabeth Elliot traveled into the Ecuadorian jungle to reach the Auca tribe with the love of Jesus. On January 8, 1956, while attempting to contact the Aucas, Jim and four other missionaries were speared to death; slain by those they came to minister to. Elisabeth, along with her 10-month-old daughter Val, would remain in the jungle for the next seven years, eventually moving into the tribal village and seeing the Aucas come to know the love of God. Later, when asked how this miraculous outcome was accomplished, Elisabeth simply replied, "I just did the next thing."

The bulk of life is extremely mundane. We wake up, brush our teeth, get dressed, go to work, do stuff, talk to people, drive home, eat, clean the dishes, brush our teeth, and go to bed. Repeat. And intermixed in this daily routine are such exploits as taking out the garbage, changing diapers, talking to more people, doing laundry, and grocery shopping. In reviewing our lives, we can easily ask, "Where is the significance?" Especially when compared to the exciting lives we see transforming the world on social media, or those we read about in biographies. But Elisabeth Elliot's life and statement ought to convey to us something quite the opposite. A life in Christ faithfully walked out in doing that next mundane thing will, in retrospect, have revealed the supernatural work of God. We may see some of it this side of eternity, but I suspect the vast majority will be revealed on the other side. So be encouraged to *"walk in the light as He is in the light"* (1 John 1:7) and just do the next thing. One step at a time.

Whatever You Have

"One of His disciples, Andrew, Simon Peter's brother, said to Him, there is a lad here who has five barley loaves and two small fish, but what are they among so many?" (John 6:8-9).

Sometimes we may fall into the trap of thinking what we have to offer is so paltry, why do it at all? This came to me yesterday as we were singing in church *"...all that I have is a hallelujah, and I know it's not much but I've nothing else fit for a King."* But it struck me—this is exactly what we are to do. Like the little boy who had a "measly" two fish and five loaves. Surely, that's not going to feed five thousand people. Even Andrew could do the math on that one.

And that's the problem when we lean on our own understanding. Two fish and five loaves for 5000+ people? It doesn't make sense. Seems illogical. Irrational. But the lad was willing to give what he had, and God did the rest. And so it is with us. Nothing is insignificant to God. When we feed, clothe, or visit one of the least of these, we do it to Jesus. The widow who gave two little coins gave more than anyone else. A cup of cold water given in Jesus' name will bring about a great reward. Yes, a cup of cold water. This is the value system of God. What we deem as no big deal, God sees as huge. For in His hands, He will multiply what we could not if it had remained in ours.

Going Toward Your Goliaths

"So it was, when the Philistine arose and came and drew near to meet David, that David hurried and ran toward the army to meet the Philistine" (1 Samuel 17:48).

The familiar story of David and Goliath is quite the contrast between the army of Israel and the young boy David (probably 16-18 years of age). Here was the army, tasked to protect the nation, and one person paralyzed them with fear by both his sound and sight:

> *"When Saul and all Israel heard these words of the Philistine, they were dismayed and greatly afraid. And all the men of Israel, when they saw the man, fled from him and were dreadfully afraid"* (1 Samuel 17:11).

In contrast, David, who heard and saw the same thing, drew quite the opposite conclusion. Confident in the size of His God, David went forward knowing the victory was assured because he had faith in His God to deliver:

> *"This day the Lord will deliver you into my hand....that all the earth may know there is a God in Israel"* (1 Samuel 17:46).

Contrary to the bumper sticker that falsely boasted "No Fear", we all fear many things. As the research of the amygdala tells us, God wisely designed us with a fear response. One lesson we can learn from this story is, our faith in the size of our God will determine our response when we are called by Him to move forward. All the thousands fighting for the army of Israel claimed allegiance to the one true God, but only one moved forward. Unbelief can be subtle, shrinking our God and expanding our fears. To the point where the writer of Hebrews warns us against *"an evil heart of unbelief in departing from the living God"* (Hebrews 3:12), for those who rejected God during the Exodus heard His Word, *"but the word which they heard did not profit them, not being mixed with faith in those who heard it"* (Hebrews 4:2).

So, let's not be like them, but let's have great faith in our great God, seeing Him (vs. our fears) for who He really is: *"Oh magnify the Lord with me, and let us exalt His name together"* (Psalm 34:3).

The Artist and His Canvas

"For we are His workmanship, created in Christ Jesus
for good works, which God prepared beforehand
that we should walk in them" (Ephesians 2:10).

In the above verse, the Greek word for "workmanship" is *poiema,* where we get our English words *"poem"* and *"poetry"*. It means that which is made, a work of art. It refers to a masterpiece, craftmanship, a handiwork, something made by hand with creative skill and ability.

"We are, not metaphorically but in very truth, a Divine work of art, something that God is making, and therefore something with which He will not be satisfied until it has a certain character... it is natural for us to wish that God had designed for us a less glorious and less arduous destiny; but then we are wishing not for more love but for less." The Problem of Pain, C.S. Lewis

"The Christian is in a different position from other people who are trying to be good. They hope, by being good, to please God if there is one; or—if they think there is not—at least they hope to deserve approval from good men. But the Christian thinks any good he does comes from the Christ-life inside him. He does not think God will love us because we are good, but that God will make us good because He loves us; just as a roof of a greenhouse does not attract the sun because it is bright, but becomes bright because the sun shines on it." Mere Christianity C.S. Lewis

Nowhere Else to Turn

"But David strengthened himself in the Lord his God"
(1 Samuel 30:6).

If you've ever lost it after being hit with extreme difficulty and affliction, fell into a pity party of "woe is me", or became enraged at those you held responsible, then you can relate to what happened to David's motley crew in 1 Samuel 30. Having been rejected in their desire to form an alliance with a neighboring country, this disappointed group returned home to find smoke rising where their city once stood, their homes in ashes, their possessions gone, and their wives and children kidnapped. The Bible says they *"wept until they had no more strength to weep"* (v. 4). And when they found the depths of their shared grief could not satisfy their intense pain, in rage they turned on David to execute the one who had led them down this disastrous path.

In no less pain than any of his men, we see here that *"David strengthened [encouraged] himself in the Lord his God."* He didn't get defensive, he didn't fight fire with fire, he didn't wallow in self-pity, nor did he vow revenge. David went to God for his strength, for he had nowhere else to turn. All other sources of strength had been stripped away. No family and no friends. All of it gone. No one wants to be in a situation like this, where there is no one to understand or help us solve our problems. But from David we learn, when all is caving in around us and there is no one else to turn to, if we turn to Him, we will find grace and strength to help us in our time of desperate need.

Leaning In

"I want you to do whatever will help you serve the Lord best, with as few distractions as possible" (1 Corinthians 7:35).

"Keep your eyes straight ahead; ignore all sideshow distractions" (Proverbs 4:25 - MSG).

Microsoft reported a while back the attention span of a human had become less than a goldfish (8 vs. 9 seconds). While this supposed study has been debunked, it's sad to think humans are now being mentioned in the same breath as goldfish. That said, if we're completely honest, it does point to something true—humans are very distracted. Living in the information age, we are bombarded daily with real-time information from around the world. Never in the 1200's did a member of an English hamlet have to sort through all this informational overload we have to process. And unlike today as I write this, no settler of the American West had to process the fatalities at a Myanmar jade mine landside, or that Sam Asghari is seeking a divorce from Britney Spears 14 months after their wedding. Granted, much of this TMI we have within our power to stop or control, but much of it I'm afraid we must just accept as part of the age in which we live.

What are we to do with all this noise? I could ask the world to please stop. But I suspect it wouldn't listen. That would have as much success as being in a noisy restaurant and going up to the manager to ask everyone to please be quiet because we can't hear the person we're with. It's not going to happen. So, what do we do in a restaurant? We lean in. We get closer and focus our attention on the person we're having a conversation with. It's the same with God. Now, more than ever in our day and age, we must lean in and make the time to focus on the One who patiently waits to give us His undivided, loving attention. Let's be like Mary who *"sat at Jesus' feet and heard His word"* (Luke 10:39), while her sister *"was distracted with much"* (Luke 10:40).

His Presence our Need

"Fear not, for I am with you" (Isaiah 41:10).

The details are sketchy now, but for approximately a month, on a nightly basis, my eight-year-old self (Steve) would cry out for my mom. With increasing decibels coupled with decreasing pauses, I would cry out "Mom!" in the darkness until she arrived in my room to reassure me she was there. What my nightlight could not accomplish, her presence could. In the same way, our God throughout Scripture constantly assures and reassures us of this one fact: *"Never will I leave you or forsake you."* He doesn't promise us victory on our terms, or safety according to our ideas of comfort, or a timeline congruent with our wishes, but what He does promise is His presence. In the darkness, when the way is difficult and makes no sense, His presence is both His provision and our light.

And what is our response to the constant relational presence of Jesus in our lives? Dependency. Reciprocity is necessary in any healthy friendship, and in Christ, our recognized need for Him forms what will ultimately create the story of our life. While a Netflix documentary on our life might mention this relationship as the backstory, to the Father and His children it is the main event. This world emphasizes achievement and checking off all on our bucket list, but the Lord defines a life well-lived in dramatically stark contrast.

Going to War

"Stand therefore, having girded your waist with truth, having put on the breastplate of righteousness, and having shod your feet with the preparation of the gospel of peace; above all, taking the shield of faith with which you will be able to quench all the fiery darts of the enemy. And take the helmet of salvation, and the sword of the Spirit, which is the word of God; praying always with all prayer and supplication in the Spirit..." (Ephesians 6:14-18).

The beach is a great place to sport some sunglasses, a t-shirt, shorts, and flip-flops. But not so much on the battlefield. That attire will ensure things end very, very poorly for you. And what's true in the physical world is also true in the spiritual world. Every day we need to dress for the war zone in which we live. For every day the Bible tells us we are in a battle over our souls. So today, lift up the shield of faith so you can extinguish all those nasty darts of condemnation, judgement, and accusation. Believe instead God's promises of His unconditional love towards you in Christ. You are adopted, and *"nothing will separate you from the love of God which is in Christ Jesus our Lord,"* (Romans 8:39) and *"If God is for you, who can be against you?"* (Romans 8:31). And grab the only offensive weapon in the above list, *"the sword of the Spirit, which is the word of God."* God's Word is powerful, in fact we are told *"the word of God is living and active and sharper than any two-edged sword"* (Hebrews 4:12). No, these are not just any words. These words are alive and powerful, enabling you to advance in life and in your soul.

So today I encourage you to dress for the occasion.

The Burdens of Life

"The Lord will perfect that which concerns me; your mercy, O Lord, endures forever; do not forsake the works of your hands"
(Psalm 138:8).

Do you have any concerns today? Perhaps a wayward child? A recent diagnosis? Or maybe you are waiting for the lab results to see if there's going to be a diagnosis? Has an unexpected bill come with no apparent means by which to pay it? Do you have a fractured relationship in need of repair? Or possibly you have aging parents, and you wonder daily what the future will bring.

Even if none of the above applies to you, we all have our own personal concerns we bear each and every day. One promise I go back to frequently is this promise found in Psalm 138. The Lord promises to perfect that which concerns me. So, I love to turn to this passage and just begin listing all of my concerns and cares to the Lord verbally in prayer. After I'm done unloading my dump truck, I then go back through each thing on the list and say, "The Lord will perfect _____". This theme is throughout Scripture, for the Lord says to *"cast all your care upon Him, for he cares for you"* (1 Peter 5:7). And we have the promise *"....that all things work together for good to those who love God, to those who are called according to His purpose"* (Romans 8:28).

You can be assured God will work *all* things together for good. Not some things. *All* things. *All* of your concerns and cares He will take and do what only God can do—He will perfect them and make them good. So don't delay. This morning, cast *all* your cares on Him for He cares for you.

How To Be Strong

"And He said to me, "My grace is sufficient for you, for My strength is made perfect in weakness." Therefore most gladly I will rather boast in my infirmities, that the power of Christ may rest upon me"
(2 Corinthians 12:9).

A paradox can be defined as "a statement containing two opposite ideas that make it seem impossible or unlikely, although it is true." The Bible is full of paradoxes. We often find in the Bible that what our human intuition thinks is the right path to a desired end is, in fact, not. For instance, take the idea of having inner strength. Conventional wisdom abounds with countless books and podcasts on how to achieve it. Yet in the Bible we're told the road to strength is paved with weakness. Why is that? It's because, for the Christian, a supernatural exchange has occurred, for it's *"no longer I who live, but Christ lives in me"* (Galatians 2:20). The shocking truth—a separate Person now living inside us—is a game changer. For the essence of the Christian life is not about morality and following a bunch of rules, but about dependence. It's not about autonomous individualism, but about humility, for *"God resists the proud but gives grace to the humble"* (1 Peter 5:5). The more we embrace our own human frailties and turn to the One who inhabits us, the stronger we will become.

That's why Paul could paradoxically conclude, *"I take pleasure in infirmities, in reproaches, in needs, in persecutions, in distresses, for Christ's sake. For when I am weak then I am strong"* (2 Corinthians 12:10). Thus, the road to confident strength is found in a power not your own. I can't, but He can. And when He does, then *"I can do all things through Christ who strengthens me"* (Philippians 4:13).

FALL

*Transitions are a time of reflection,
and a time for looking forward.*
Roy Cooper

*It is the difficult, painful transitions that can yield
the greatest understanding of purpose in our lives.*
Arthur C. Brooks

Transitions

FALL is a season here in the Pacific Northwest where we can watch the trees change before our very eyes! I never grow tired of seeing the trees move from green to gold to red and then ultimately to empty! As I drive around my city during this season, observing the beauty of the changing trees inevitably draws my eyes upwards. I find myself praising God for creating such beauty for us to enjoy.

Steve, on the other hand, doesn't necessarily enjoy the barrage of leaves that find their way to our lawn during this season! He is outside many times with the leaf-blower trying to stay ahead of the changing trees.

Isn't that the way life can be sometimes too? We have a sense that change is coming. Sometimes we can almost see it hurtling towards us and maybe we try to get out ahead of the change, but it will come no matter what we do.

FALL is the great signal of transition. As calendars go, we are all getting ready for the cold blast of WINTER temperatures. But FALL also brings with it great reasons to celebrate the change of seasons. Many school-age children are going back to their academic pursuits. Along with school starting comes FALL sports. I, for one, definitely enjoy college football, and I am quite the fanatic for my own team!

FALL ushers in family gatherings like Thanksgiving, a great reminder to live each day in gratitude. So even though FALL reminds us of how difficult transition and change can be, the beauty of the turning trees, the return to a school-type schedule, and reasons to gather in community, are also reminders to be grateful for it all. God is the Author and Finisher of our faith, and His Word is the book of life, the manual of the soul, the textbook of salvation, and the most precious thing in the whole universe. His Word provides us with hope, no matter our season.

Classroom Management

"For we have no power against this great multitude that is coming against us; nor do we know what to do, but our eyes are upon You"
(2 Chronicles 20:12).

With all due respect to the Gregorian calendar, if you're a parent of school-aged children, the start of the new year is about to begin. And if you are a teacher of those who are just starting out their education, it's so important to establish "law and order" that very first week. Children being children, chaos and disorder are just around the corner if we leave them to their own devices. One method I've seen teachers deploy on those who are on the verge of rioting is "1, 2, 3, eyes on me." I have personally witnessed rooms on the precipice of mob rule come to silent attention as they fix their eyes on the one who has exerted their control of the classroom by means of this directive.

In many ways, a child's classroom is a microcosm of our world. And sometimes even our own souls. Not only does it seem our world is daily engulfed with chaos and disorder, but our own lives and souls can often feel so completely out of control too. And to complicate matters, like Jehoshaphat in the verse above, our ability to extrapolate negative outcomes into our future overlays fear into our present. What's a child of God to do? In the classroom of life, our Teacher is calling out, "1, 2, 3, eyes on Me". *"But my eyes are upon You, O God the Lord; In You I take refuge"* (Psalm 141:8). While He may not deliver you *from* the chaos of life, when we look away and look up to Him, our sovereign Lord will *be* our order in it.

Psalm 91

With apologies to those with absolutely no interest, in honor of the NFL start of the season in September, I would like to remind you (all you extreme NFL fans) of the "Psalm 91" shirt Ray Lewis wore after the Baltimore Ravens won the Super Bowl in 2013. A favorite psalm of believers for thousands of years, it speaks of the many benefits we receive when we abide in His presence. Now what's interesting about the psalm are the references to God. They go from a second (You) and third (He) person point of view in verses 1-13, to a first person (I) point of view in verses 14-16. Meaning, God suddenly begins talking to us directly in these verses. And because we know all the promises in the Bible have personal application for the Christian, we each can personally enter into and receive these truths for our own lives. So, I invite you to insert your name into this passage and believe this to be true for your life:

> Because _____ has set his/her love upon Me,
> therefore I will deliver _____;
> I will set _____ on high, because _____ has known My name.
> _____ shall call upon Me, and I will answer _____.
> I will be with _____ in trouble;
> I will deliver _____ and honor _____.
> With long life I will satisfy _____, and show _____ My salvation.

If you have set your love upon God, your Father wants to speak directly to you today. And every day hereafter.

Being Thankful

"Enter into His gates with thanksgiving and into His courts with praise. Be thankful to Him, and bless His name. For the Lord is good; His mercy is everlasting, and His truth endures to all generations"
(Psalm 100:4-5).

As a lifelong Seattleite, I've noticed how prone we are to complain about the weather. When it's cold or rainy, we wish it was hotter. And when it gets hotter, it's too hot and we long for cooler days. The Israelites, as they departed Egypt for the promised land, were just like us. Only three days after seeing the miracle of the Red Sea parting, they were already complaining about their newfound life in the desert. *"And the people complained against Moses...."* (Exodus 15:24). Moses responds by providing us insight into the fundamental nature of complaint when he says, *"...for the Lord hears your complaints which you make against Him. And what are we? Your complaints are not against us but against the Lord"* (Exodus 16:8).

Gratitude is a choice and an act of the will. It's the answer to the question: By which lens will I see and interpret the world and my experience in it? For all that has, is, or will be good in my life, will I recognize Him as the source? *"Do not be deceived, my beloved brethren. Every good gift and every perfect gift is from above, and comes down from the Father of lights"* (James 1:16-17). And further, how will I define what a "good gift" is? Will I see it only according to the major events of life, or will I be able to see it in good coffee, indoor plumbing, duct tape, invisible antibodies, Wi-Fi, deodorant, GPS, cute puppies, oxygen, and a hot shower? The more we give thanks, the more we see to be thankful for. And even then, when it's all said and done, when we've exhausted all the things we can possibly be thankful for, I suspect all we've really done is capture a tiny teacup under the Niagara Falls of God's goodness to us.

Singing and Rejoicing with Gladness

"The Lord your God is in your midst, the Mighty One, will save; He will rejoice over you with gladness, He will quiet you with His love, He will rejoice over you with singing" (Zephaniah 3:17).

"The Lord your God is in your midst"

You can have joy today, and every day, because you are not alone in anything you do. He is powerfully in you, your mortal and frail body now a receptacle of our immortal and all-loving God.

"the Mighty One, will save"

You can have faith today because the Mighty One redeemed and saved you, and now He can be trusted to always save you from the next peril to be faced.

"He will rejoice over you with gladness"

You can have joy today because you are not a mistake or failure in His eyes, but are loved just as you are, created because your God longed to have relationship with you.

"He will quiet you with His love"

You can have peace today in His presence, no matter the situation, for He is able to calm the areas of anxiety and stress by freeing you with the depths of His affections.

"He will rejoice over you with singing."

The word *"rejoice"* means to be joyful and jubilant because of a triumph or success. You can find rest today because your God sees you already as a triumph, for Jesus Christ *"disarmed principalities and powers, making a public spectacle of them, triumphing over them in the cross"* (Colossians 2:15), and you are now a participant in the triumph and success of Christ. So today, may you allow God to love and sing over that which you have deemed unlovable all your life.

Choose Joy

"Rejoice in the Lord always. Again I will say, rejoice!"
(Philippians 4:4).

In 2023, the Oklahoma Sooner women's softball team won their third straight national championship, having won a record 53 games in a row. Afterwards, an ESPN reporter asked the three leaders of the team how they maintained their joy as a team as they handled the pressure and anxiety, given the high expectations placed upon them throughout the year. To a player, they each expressed the same unexpected source. The Sooners captain Grace Lyons kicked it off by saying,

> "The only way you can have a joy that doesn't fade away is from the Lord. Any other joy is actually happiness, which comes from circumstances and outcomes. Joy in the Lord is the only thing that can keep you motivated regardless of the outcomes. There's no way softball will ever bring you that given how much failure there is in it, and how much of a rollercoaster the game can be."

Next, Jayda Coleman said,

> "What makes our team so strong is we're not afraid to lose. It's not the end of the world if we do lose because our life is in Christ, and that's all that matters."

And finally, Alyssa Brito wrapped it up with,

> "We're fixing our eyes on Christ. You can't find your fulfillment in an outcome, whether good or bad. It brings so much freedom to live for the Kingdom, to play for something bigger, and to love one another. This isn't our home, because we have an eternity of joy ahead with our Father and King."

As believers filled with Christ, whether we are on the mountaintop of yet another national championship, or in the valley of a hot, filthy, Roman prison cell where a chained Paul wrote to the Philippians, we can always choose joy.

He is Able

"And not being weak in faith, Abraham did not consider his own body, already dead (since he was about a hundred years old), and the deadness of Sarah's womb. He did not waver at the promise of God through unbelief, but was strengthened in faith, giving glory to God, and being fully convinced that what He had promised He was also able to perform" (Romans 4:19-21).

In my youth, I would have defined *faith* as "believing in something you know isn't true." What I've come to realize is the quality of our faith is only as good as the object in which it is placed. I can have great faith a paper chair will hold me up, but in the end, I'll find myself flat on my back. Conversely, I can worry and fret a solid steel chair won't hold me up, but lo and behold, in the end I find that it does. And in fact, given the construction standards in America, I would say we all have "great faith" when it comes to sitting in chairs. I see minimal worry, fear, or anxiety when I observe people in public sitting down in chairs. That's because chairs have a good track record, and we remember their faithfulness.

So, faith is all about its object—is it faithful? This then was the test Abraham and Sarah had before them when God said they would have a son. Would they believe the facts of being well beyond their childbearing years, or would they believe the promise of God? In the hierarchy of what is ultimately true, which is to be more trusted—the facts as we perceive them, or what God has said?

Our God is faithful. He keeps His promises, and so He is worthy of our trust. Regardless of what the "facts" may be saying to you, walk by faith and not by sight. Believe His Word, for it is an anvil that has worn out (and will wear out) many hammers.

No Accident

*"And He has made from one blood every nation of men
to dwell on all the face of the earth, and has determined
their preappointed times and the boundaries of their dwellings,
so that they should seek the Lord" (Acts 17:26-27).*

With God there is no Plan B. He never impotently wrings His metaphorical hands in heaven pondering, "Oh no, now what do I do?" Our infinite God is always in complete control, while simultaneously allowing His finite creation the free agency to do as they wish. Take for instance the death of Christ. Here we see God's sovereignty and man's responsibility working hand in hand. Two sides of the single coin—*"Him [Jesus], being delivered by the determined purpose and foreknowledge of God, you have taken by lawless hands, have crucified, and put to death"* (Acts 2:23). God's sovereignty and human accountability working in tandem. One not nullifying the other.

With that as the backdrop, see the truth Paul is communicating to the Athenians in Acts 17:26-27.......and to us today. Consider the year you were born. That was no accident. God in His sovereignty brought you into the world at the exact preappointed time. For your purpose and His. But He didn't stop there. Not only was the year you were born established *"by the determined purpose and foreknowledge of God"*, but so is your current geographical placement. The exact location of your current address has not been relegated to random chance. Time and space have been preappointed for you and every baby ever born. Why? *"...so that they should seek the Lord."* This is why you were born when you were born, and this is why you are where you are.

It Is Well With My Soul

*"I have told you these things, so that in Me you may have peace.
In this world you will have trouble. But take heart!
I have overcome the world" (John 16:33).*

On November 21, 1873, Anna Spafford and her four young daughters set sail from the U.S. to Europe on the French ocean liner, Ville du Havre. About four days into the crossing the ship collided with the Scottish ship, the Loch Earn. Within approximately 12 minutes, the Ville du Havre slipped beneath the dark waters of the Atlantic, carrying with it 226 of the 313 passengers, including the four Spafford children. A sailor, rowing a small boat over the spot where the ship went down, spotted a woman floating on a piece of wreckage. It was Anna, still alive. Nine days later she arrived in Cardiff, Wales and immediately wired her husband Horatio, "Saved alone, what shall I do?"

Horatio booked passage on the next available ship and left to join his grieving wife. With the ship about four days out, the captain called Spafford to his cabin and told him they were over the place where his children went down. It was then that Mr. Spafford returned to his cabin and wrote the following hymn:

*When peace like a river attendeth my way,
when sorrows like sea billows roll –
Whatever my lot,
Thou hast taught me to say,
It is well, it is well with my soul.*

*Though Satan should buffet,
though trials should come,
let this blest assurance control,
that Christ hath regarded my helpless estate,
and has shed His own blood for my soul.*

*My sin, oh the bliss of this glorious thought,
my sin not in part but the whole,
is nailed to the cross
and I bear it no more,
Praise the Lord, Praise the Lord, O my soul!*

*And Lord, haste the day when my faith shall be sight,
the clouds be rolled back as a scroll:
The trump shall resound,
and the Lord shall descend,
even so, it is well with my soul!*

Change

"I the Lord do not change" (Malachi 3:6).

Nothing stays the same. The hot weather of SUMMER is now becoming a distant memory. The current news cycle is not what it was a week ago. People in our lives come and go, we're subject to ever-changing moods and emotions, and hair that was once was abundant and colored, is now sparse and gray. And for us older folks with aging bodies, like the song says, "the old gray mare she ain't what she used to be." Change is the one thing that doesn't change.

Isn't it wonderful to wake up every morning and know our immutable God hasn't changed? *"God is love."* The God who loved you unconditionally yesterday loves you to the same degree today. *"When we are faithless, He remains faithful" (2 Timothy 2:13),* for *"Jesus Christ is the same yesterday, today, and forever"* (Hebrews 13:8). May all of life's disappointing variations point us to the true and only Source of stability in this crazy world. Be strong and courageous in the ever-shifting ebbs and flows of life, for His promises contained in the Bible are an anchor for the soul.

Where are the other nine?

"...there met Him ten men who were lepers, who stood afar off. And they lifted up their voices and said, 'Jesus, Master, have mercy on us!' He said to them, 'Go, show yourselves to the priests.' And so it was that as they went, they were cleansed. And one of them.... returned, and with a loud voice glorified God, and fell down on his face at His feet, giving Him thanks. So, Jesus answered and said, "Were there not ten cleansed? But where are the other nine?"
(Luke 17:12-17).

We take so much for granted. When the power goes out, I'm sure many of us realize just how much we take heat, lighting, and refrigeration for granted. And maybe that's why the other nine didn't return to say, "thank you." Or maybe they thought, "I'll do it later, when it's more convenient." Or "God already knows my heart, so why bother going all the way back when He already knows how grateful I am?" Or maybe they weren't grateful at all, feeling their healing was an inalienable right, and was deserved much earlier in the life and ministry of Jesus. That could be entirely possible, for the garden of ingratitude is often watered with our pride.

Whatever the reason, we know only one of the ten returned to give thanks to the Source of their healing. From this recorded history, we learn several lessons about gratitude. One, it is physical. The cleansed leper *"returned".* Two, it is communicated, either in writing or verbally, for he was *"giving Him thanks."* And finally, gratitude is always extended to a person. In this case, Jesus. God did not design the world for us to give thanks to inanimate objects, but instead to people and to the One who created them. So, I guess in the end we'll never really know why the other nine didn't return, but let's be the one who does.

Our Happy Place

"The eternal God is your refuge" (Deuteronomy 33:27).

Everyone needs a happy place. A place of safety and restoration, where one can be refreshed, encouraged, and built up as we go through the numerous trials of life. While many of us have unfortunately experienced the exact opposite, our homes should be such havens of happiness. The above Hebrew word translated *refuge* appears twice in the Old Testament, and can also be translated *mansion, abode, habitation,* or *dwelling place.* This conveys the thought that *God is our home.* This is a beautiful metaphor; for while our homes are dear to us, far greater still is our loving God, *"in whom we live and move and have our being"* (Acts 17:28). We find in God all that is good about home.

In our homes we feel safe. Gone is the noise of the day as we dwell in quiet security and peace. In the same way, when we are with our God, we *"fear no evil"* (Psalm 23:4), for He is our hiding place, shelter, and retreat. At home we rest after a hard day of work. And so, our hearts find rest in God. When we grow weary, we turn to Him and our souls dwell at ease. At home we can let our hair down and be ourselves, no longer afraid of being misunderstood or our words being misconstrued. So, with God we can be our true and authentic selves, open and honest with the One who accepts us just as we are. And finally, in our homes we find our true and purest happiness, and it's in God that our hearts find their deepest delight. Maybe you've never experienced a home like I've described, but God is that home for you, for He is your Home Sweet Home.

His Presence

"You will show me the path of life; in your presence is fullness of joy,
at your right hand are pleasures forevermore" (Psalm 16:11).

A fun 1981 Hollywood adventure movie, *Raiders of the Lost Ark*, pitted the beloved archeology professor Indiana Jones against the German Third Reich in a race to find the legendary Ark of the Covenant, believing it had supernatural powers to wipe out entire armies. If I remember the grand finale correctly, the two bad guys open the Ark and, after some scary looking ghosts fly around for a few seconds, their faces melt in some incredible pre-CGI animation. Now I'm not one to develop my theology from the movie industry, but it has made me wonder what it must be like to be in the presence of God.

In Christ, the Bible encourages us to *"come boldly into God's presence"* (Hebrews 4:16), and He promises us that *"My presence shall go with you and I will give you rest"* (Exodus 33:14).

David had a solitary request:

> *"One thing I have desired of the Lord, that will I seek: That I may dwell in the house of the Lord all the days of my life, to behold the beauty of the Lord, and to inquire in His temple"* (Psalm 27:4).

And we are instructed to *"come before His presence with thanksgiving; let us shout joyfully to Him with psalms"* (Psalm 95:2).

As His adopted child, here's what it's like being in the presence of your Heavenly Father: there's fullness of joy, pleasures forever, there's boldness (vs. fear) in approaching Him, there's plenty of rest (vs. work) with Him, we can ask Him questions, it's beautiful, you'll want to be near Him all day, you'll find so much to be grateful for, and joyful singing will abound.

So, seek His presence. I promise your face will not melt, and you'll find the more you experience His presence, the more you will want it.

Good Historians

"I will remember the years of the right hand of the Most High.
I will remember the works of the Lord; surely
I will remember Your wonders of old" (Psalm 77:10-11).

"Bless the Lord, O my soul, and forget not all His benefits"
(Psalm 103:2).

Our memory and what we remember (or don't remember) is a very tricky thing. Some things we'd like to forget but can't (the pain of the past), while other things we can't remember (Where did I put my keys? What's her name again?). And as one who personally knows, I can attest that age certainly does not improve one's ability to remember. And yet, God calls us to be good historians. Why is that? Over time, as we walk with the Lord, we will begin to see a pattern of His faithfulness in the rearview mirror of life. That pattern, because *"Jesus is the same yesterday, today, and forever"* (Hebrews 13:8), is the confidence and assurance that what we see ahead in the windshield of life will be met with the same faithfulness. This is what faith is. We grow in our faith not only when we trust what we read in the Bible is true (despite what we may feel, see, or hear), but also when we believe the great faithfulness we've seen from Him in the past will occur in our future.

So, let's be good historians, remembering how faithful our God has been to us over the years. As we sang yesterday in church,

"All my life You have been faithful,
and all my life You have been so, so good.
With every breath that I am able,
I will sing of the goodness of God."

God Wants Us to Complain

"I cry out to the Lord with my voice; with my voice to the Lord I make my supplication. I pour out my complaint before Him; I declare before Him my trouble" (Psalm 142:1-2).

In the movie *Saving Private Ryan*, we are provided with some surprising insight when it comes to griping and complaining—gripes go *up* (YouTube has a clip of the interaction if you've not seen the movie). The principle is this—when you complain down to others, it brings you (and them) down. When you complain up to God, He lifts you up. Now Jesus said, *"In this world you will have tribulation,* but He also said, *"take heart; I have overcome the world"* (John 16:33). To help us in overcoming the world, God has been gracious to give us what are called *psalms of lament*. About one third of the psalms in the Bible are psalms of lament. For example, you have psalms about sorrow (137), anger (140), fear (69), longing (85), confusion (102), desolation (22) repentance (51), disappointment (74), and depression (88), to name just a few.

This implies God expects us to frequently feel and experience pain in the normal course of living, and therefore frequently express our pain to Him. He wants us to tell Him exactly how we feel—*"my spirit was overwhelmed within me....there is no one who acknowledges me, no one cares for my soul"* (Psalm 142:3-4), while also having a spirit of faith and trust that He will provide—*"For You shall deal bountifully with me"* (Psalm 142:7). The psalms of lament model for us how to complain to God in a way that honors Him. They are expressions of God's compassion for us, because in them we see we are not alone in our feelings, and that God does indeed care and understand. To study more about being a faith-full complainer, I encourage you to read, study, and meditate on these psalms of lament.

Eyes to See

*"Therefore I speak to them in parables, because seeing they do not
see, and hearing they do not hear, nor do they understand.
But blessed are your eyes for they see, and your ears for they hear"
(Matthew 13:13,16).*

Fanny J Crosby was born in New York in 1820, and at six weeks of age, a treatment for an inflammation of her eyes blinded her for life. When she died nearly 95 years later, she had written between 5,500 and 9,000 hymns, the exact count being obscured by the numerous pseudonyms (up to 200) she employed, as publishers were hesitant to have so many hymns by one person in their hymnals. On several occasions, upon hearing an unfamiliar hymn sung, she would inquire about the author only to find it to be one of her own. "Blindness," she wrote in later life, "cannot keep the sunlight of hope from the trustful soul."

As Jesus said, eyesight does not guarantee vision. And conversely, the blindness of Fanny Crosby only enhanced her ability to see the unseen. This counterintuitive miracle can only be explained by the resurrecting life and power of Jesus Christ, the One who alone can raise the dead and enable the blind to see. Later in life, when a pastor lamented God had not granted her sight, Fanny replied, "Do you know that if at birth I had been able to make one petition, it would have been that I was born blind? Because when I get to heaven, the first face that shall ever gladden my sight will be that of my Savior."

From the hymn, *Blessed Assurance:*

> *Perfect submission, all is at rest,*
> *I in my Savior am happy and blest;*
> *Watching and waiting, looking above,*
> *filled with His goodness, lost in His love.*
>
> *This is my story, this is my song,*
> *praising my Savior all the day long;*
> *This is my story, this is my song,*
> *praising my Savior all the day long.*

Good Medicine

*"A good, but unexamined life will be high on duty and
not likely to celebrate the odd paradoxes, the ironic coincidences,
and the humor of being dirt." C. S. Lewis*

*"A merry heart does good, like medicine,
but a broken spirit dries the bones" (Proverbs 17:22).*

Many studies have shown laughter boosts your immune system, increases endorphins to your brain, eases anxiety, combats stress and increases your overall physical and mental health. But alas, where can we find humor in a world that has apparently gone so mad? Where are all these "odd paradoxes" and "ironic coincidences" C.S. Lewis talked about? Do we need to travel far or pay great sums of money to find laughter and humor? Fortunately, the answer is a resounding "NO!". It's all around you. Every day. Just ask any of your favorite comedians (insert Nate Bargatze and Jerry Seinfeld here).

Yes, and even at work. *Especially* at work. And especially if the work you do is extremely heavy and burdensome. The one requirement C.S. Lewis wisely points out will be the examined life. So, let's keep living that life, performing our duties, but also celebrating with laughter the humor of it all. Not at anyone's expense, but in the oddities and ironies of daily life together with your co-workers. Keep putting the fun into dysfunction, even as you strive for excellence in all that you and your company does. Recognizing there's often a thin line between crying and laughing. So, to the degree you can, and when appropriate, celebrate the comedy relief you so desperately need for your own (and others') physical and mental health.

Praising Him in the Pain

*"After striking them many times with the rods, they threw them into prison, commanding the jailer to guard them securely. He, having received such a strict command, threw them into the **inner prison** and fastened their feet in the stocks **in an agonizing position**. But about midnight when Paul and Silas were praying and singing hymns of praise to God, and the prisoners were listening to them, suddenly there was a great earthquake, so powerful that the very foundations of the prison were shaken and at once all the doors were opened and everyone's chains were unfastened" (Acts 16:23-26 (Amplified)).*

Studies have shown praising and worshiping our Creator provides therapeutic healing of our souls, something we all so desperately need. On a very regular basis. Now, when life is going great and you're on the mountaintop, it's fairly easy to break out into these songs of praise and thanksgiving. But what about when you are in the valley? What about when you're thrown and trapped in that *"inner prison"* or find yourself *"in an agonizing position,"* whether it be physical, or an imprisonment within the mind?

We've all been there. In fact, some of you may be there today. And if you're not there today, someday you will be. Paul and Silas were there. And what was their response? In the inner prison, in their agonizing position, they praised their God. In the pain. In the trial. *Before* there was any hope of deliverance. As believers, when we praise God in the pain, when we respond with prayer and praise in the prison, we not only find ourselves changed, but we powerfully influence those who are watching and listening. Such is the power of prayer and praise. These spiritual weapons open closed doors, break chains, and set prisoners free.

Reflecting on Romans 8:28

"And we know that all things work together for good to those who love God, to those who are called according to His purpose"
(Romans 8:28).

This past week a family close to ours lost a baby girl at birth. The perfectly healthy baby had complications during the birthing process, and two days later she passed away. So much grief, and so many tears. What words of consolation will bring solace to the heartbroken mother who walks alone into her little girl's empty nursery room? There are no words. We weep with those who weep. I've spent time this week reflecting on the pain and suffering we experience in life, reading the Bible and the writings of Randy Alcorn, and praying for this grieving family. So, I'd like to spend the next few days sharing some of the wisdom I've learned from others far wiser than myself. Those who have experienced suffering, and probed deeply into the problem of pain, the Bible, and specifically Romans 8:28.

Randy Alcorn states there are two essential points we must understand about this familiar verse frequently used in the wrong way at the wrong time (the first point I'll mention now, and the second tomorrow). This verse is a statement of fact about believers, *"those who love God, to those who are called according to His purpose."* This verse is intended only for those in Christ, as the very next verse speaks of being *"conformed into the image of His Son."* Alcorn states unbelievers "cannot possibly understand its significance, and are likely to gain from it a perverted view of God, or an image of the Christian faith being a naïve game of 'let's pretend everything is rosy, even when the roof caves in.'" As believers, we have been gifted an eternal perspective that incorporates heaven, *"Therefore we do not give up....For our momentary light affliction is producing for us an absolutely incomparable eternal weight of glory. So, we do not focus on what is seen, but on what is unseen. For what is seen is temporary, but what is unseen is eternal"* (2 Corinthians 4:16-18).

Faith is believing today what one day, in retrospect, we will see has been true all along.

Reflecting on Romans 8:28 (continued)

*"And we know that all things work together for good to those
who love God, to those who are the called according to His purpose"
(Romans 8:28).*

The second crucial point about this verse is the focus is not on isolated events, but on the sum total of all events. The difference is tremendous between saying "each thing by itself is good" and "all things work together for good". The verse does not tell me I should say "it is good" if my car is stolen, my leg breaks, I'm diagnosed with cancer, my house burns down, or my child dies. But it does say God will use these events and weave them together with every other facet of my life in order to produce what He knows to be the very best for me.

Randy Alcorn shares when he was a child, his mother would bake delicious cakes. Her routine was to lay all the ingredients out on the kitchen counter. One day he decided to try an experiment and taste each individual ingredient of the cake. Surely if the cake tasted great, so would each individual ingredient. Baking powder. Shortening. Baking soda. Flour. Raw eggs. Vanilla extract. Even the semi-sweet chocolate tasted bitter compared to the sweet milk chocolate he was used to. He discovered almost everything that went into her cakes tasted terrible by itself. But a remarkable metamorphosis took place when his mother, far more knowledgeable and wiser and skilled than he was, mixed the ingredients in just the right amounts and baked them together at just the right temperature for just the right amount of time.

In the same way, the individual ingredients of trials and tragedies that come into our lives are not initially "delicious" nor desirable. In fact, they often are very bitter. And so, God does not ask us to immediately see every individual event as wonderful. But He does expect us to trust He is sovereignly at work even in that event and will use it in concert with everything else for our very best good.

Reflecting on Romans 8:28 (continued)

"And we know that all things work together for good to those
who love God, to those who are the called according to His purpose"
(Romans 8:28).

On July 30, 1967, 17-year-old Joni Eareckson Tada dove into Chesapeake Bay. Misjudging the depth of the water, she fractured her cervical vertebrae and became a quadriplegic, paralyzed from the shoulders down. During her two years of rehabilitation, Joni experienced extreme anger, deep depression, and desperately wanted to end her life. Over five decades later she writes this about Romans 8:28:

> "But what about those two wonderful, perplexing words *all things*? In his second letter to the Corinthians, Paul lists some of the experiences he includes under that heading. Severe floggings. Staring death in the face. Bloody lashings with a whip. Brutal beatings with rods. Terrifying shipwrecks. Danger from bandits. Heartaches over betrayals and false believers. Exposure, exhaustion, hunger, and thirst (2 Corinthians 11:23-28). And the list goes on. Most of us would say that our problems pale in light of Paul's list. Yet he could still write, "I *know* that in *all things* God works for my good" (emphasis mine). What's keeping you from believing in God's goodness right now, in the midst of your difficulties, pressures, and disappointments?"

As Joni has stated elsewhere, "God permits what He hates to achieve what He loves."

Reflecting on Romans 8:28 (continued)

"And we know that all things work together for good to those
who love God, to those who are the called according to His purpose"
(Romans 8:28).

Benjamin B. Warfield is a world-renowned theologian who taught at Princeton Seminary for thirty-four years. When twenty-five, he married Annie Kinkead and they traveled to Germany for their honeymoon. While there, during an intense thunderstorm, she was struck by lightning and was permanently paralyzed. For the next thirty-nine years until her death, Warfield cared for Annie, seldom leaving his home for more than two hours at a time during all those years of marriage. Imagine how this event, occurring on your honeymoon, might affect your world view. This is what Warfield had to say about Romans 8:28:

> "The fundamental thought is the universal government of God. All that comes to you is under His controlling hand. The secondary thought is the favor of God to those that love Him. If He governs all, then nothing but good can befall those to whom He would do good.... Though we are too weak to help ourselves and too blind to ask for what we need, and can only groan in unformed longings, He is the author in us of these very longings...and He will so govern all things that we shall reap only good from all that befalls us."

Only good from *all* that befalls us. Benjamin Warfield spoke not from the sidelines, in the ivory tower of academia, but from the arena of pain and suffering.

Dental Care

"What do people mean when they say, 'I am not afraid of God because I know He is good'? Have they never even been to a dentist?
C. S. Lewis

"No discipline is fun while it lasts, but it seems painful at the time. Later, however, it yields the peaceful fruit of righteousness for those who have been trained by it" (Hebrews 12:11).

Recently I had the pleasure of having a root canal. I believe I'm in the majority in saying I don't get very excited when I see a dental appointment coming up. Do you? Say on par with the anticipation of a good meal, a vacation, or time devoted to your favorite hobby? I didn't think so. And yet consider a world without the dental profession. While there might be an initial collective sigh of relief, I imagine in the end there'd be a great outcry and we'd soon see dentistry return. Why? Because of the pain.

Our Heavenly Father is good. And He is love. Because He is both, He disciplines us. *"The Lord disciplines those He loves"* (Hebrews 12:6). Not punitively, for that's just punishment for the sake of punishment. But instead to nudge us in a different direction, or in some cases, to do a complete about-face. And yes, this redirection is painful. But only temporarily. The alternative would be to leave us to our own devices, encountering a far more permanent and destructive pain, one that *"kills, steals, and destroys"* (John 10:10). So, our Loving Father, our Gentle Dentist, gives us Novocain, performs His procedure, and then sets us free to recover so we can enjoy being pain free once again. Until our next dental appointment.

Distracted

"The Lord would speak to Moses face to face, as one speaks to a friend. Then Moses would return to the camp, but his young aide Joshua son of Nun did not leave the tent" (Exodus 33:11).

When Moses left, Joshua chose to linger. Now, if you've ever attempted to linger alone in the presence of God, you know how quickly distractions come. And if you try this in the morning, once that first cup of caffeine starts to kick in, suddenly you'll find yourself having the urge to check the news, take a peek at the weather, do a wash, clean out the lint in the dryer, make the bed, and reply to your many emails. And a few hundred other things. How prone we are to be like Martha, who *"was distracted with much serving,"* while her sister Mary lingered *"at Jesus' feet and heard His word"* (Luke 10:39-41).

The seventh-century English poet John Donne expressed this all too familiar human tendency when he wrote,

> "A memory of yesterday's pleasures, a fear of tomorrow's dangers, a straw under my knee, a noise in my ear, a light in mine eye, an anything, a nothing, a fancy, a chimera [or fantasy] in my brain troubles me in my prayer."

One practical approach to wandering thoughts is to keep a notepad nearby and just write them down. And then move on... until the next stray thought comes... and write that one down too. Unfortunately, this battle we all have with distractions will probably be a lifelong dilemma. But let's not succumb to them when focused, meaningful time in His presence is so needed for the health of our souls.

Hang in There

"Dear brothers, is your life full of difficulties and temptations? Then be happy, for when the way is rough, your patience has a chance to grow. So let it grow, and don't try to squirm out of your problems. For when your patience is finally in full bloom, then you will be ready for anything, strong in character, full and complete"
(James 1:2-4 -TLB).

Personally, when I wake up in the morning, I'd like a life full of ease, fun, and convenience. And when I think of happiness, I think of sleeping in, eating ice cream, and enjoying my favorite hobbies and leisure activities. Which makes me wonder about my core values and interests when I read about God's in James chapter one. It seems when life is full of difficulties and temptations, when it's rough and filled with problems, that's when we are to be happy. So happy, in fact, that we ought not to try and squirm out of them, but to patiently stay in them so it (patience) can make us strong, full, and complete. While our microwave culture views patience as extremely passive, to God it is the catalyst for supernatural activity.

Life is hard. It is filled with obstacles, resistance, and hardships. And yet, in the midst of all we will ever experience this side of eternity, He is with us. So, there's no need to try and squirm out of your problems. Jesus not only is Lord of the storm(s) you are in, but has promised to be *"with you always, even to the end of the age"* (Matthew 28:20). As Henry Blackaby, a noted Christian author and pastor has said, *"Christ will lead you into many situations that will seem impossible, but don't try to avoid them. Stay in the middle of them, for that is where you will experience God."*

Construction Zone

"And the temple, when it was being built, was built with stone finished at the quarry, so that no hammer or chisel or any iron tool was heard in the temple while it was being built" (1 Kings 6:7).

If you've ever worked or lived near a construction site, you know how loud it can be: jackhammers, drilling, hammering, excavating, and concrete joint cutting. But when the temple of the Old Testament was built, all the real construction of the temple was done in an off-site quarry. Once the stones actually reached the site where the temple was to be erected, no construction noise was heard, nor was it even necessary. The work had already been done, and now prepared; the stones could be arranged and fit together in relative silence.

I believe God wants us to understand a spiritual reality from this. The temple, we learn in the New Testament, was a copy of heaven itself (Hebrews 9:23-24). Today, you and I live in that off-site quarry called earth, for we are *"living stones, that God is building into His spiritual temple"* (1 Peter 2:5). In this quarry, as living stones, we feel the pain of the constant hammering and the heavy blows of the chisel and shaping tools. As such, we are being formed and fashioned for heaven. But to be free from pain and suffering is not life in the quarry. Someday life will be pain-free, sorrow-free, and trouble-free, but that day is not today. Let the Master Builder form you as a living stone, and when the construction is complete, you will be perfectly fitted into the heavenly temple only He can construct.

Limitless

"How often they...grieved Him in the desert!
Yes, again and again they...limited the Holy One of Israel.
They did not remember His power" (Psalm 78:40-42).

How sadly ironic the creation, made in the image of their Creator, can so quickly reverse the Divine order and shape an imaginary creator fashioned from our own human image. Take for instance our limitations. Our lives have a beginning, middle, and end. Without water, oxygen, food, or sleep, we perish. Our physical and mental capabilities cap out at some point, and in the end we recognize our best abilities still fall incredibly short of perfection. And so surely God must be like us. Limited. Powerless. Unable to do what we are unable to do, solve, think, or conceive.

The problem with limiting the Holy One of Israel is that He will become who we believe He is. This is the peril of unbelief. When Jesus was rejected by those in Nazareth, we're told *"He did not do many mighty works there because of their unbelief"* (Matthew 13:58). Elsewhere, when a distraught father cried out to Jesus concerning his son, *"If you can do anything, have compassion on us and help us"*, Jesus corrected him by responding, *"If you can believe, all things are possible to him who believes"* (Mark 9:22-23). And this is why God places such a premium on faith. Do you take Me at my word? Do you trust Me? Do you believe I am able? That is why we are called *believers*. And this is why we need to come together and stir one another's faith up, for *"...without faith it is impossible to please Him, for he who comes to God must believe that He is, and that He is a rewarder of those who diligently seek Him"* (Hebrews 11:6).

Which is it?

"In everything give thanks, for this is the will of God in Christ Jesus for you" (1 Thessalonians 5:18).

As a natural born pessimist and cynic, all my (Steve) life I've had to do battle with these unfortunate character qualities. Years ago, when I reflected deeply on the simple (but profound) metaphor of the glass (is it half full or half empty?), something clicked. So, when a former co-worker sent this to me, its simplicity and profundity resonated as I hope it will with you:

> Have you ever stopped to think that every burden we face is due to a blessing? If you have dirty dishes in the sink, it means you had food to eat. If you have a load of laundry to be washed, it means you have clothes to wear. If your car needs repair, it means you have transportation and places to go. If you fall and scrape your knees, it means you were walking around on your legs. If you're grieving the loss of a friend, it means you have loved and been loved. If you have toys scattered across your floor, it means you have little ones to enjoy and influence.

> It's so easy to see only the burdens of life. We all have them. But we should never fail to remember and give thanks for the blessings. It is the blessings that make the burdens bearable.

Now Thank We All Our God

A Thanksgiving Day reflection from Nancy DeMoss Wolgemuth:

Martin Rinkart was a 17th century Lutheran pastor serving in his hometown of Eilenberg during the height of the Thirty Years' War. A walled city, Eilenberg soon found itself overrun with refugees and injured troops, bringing on not only fear and overcrowding but a deadly wave of disease, pestilence, hunger, and want. The Rinkart home became a makeshift refuge of sorts for many of the sick and stranded. And though limited with hardly enough food and supplies to care for his own family, Martin ministered tirelessly to the needs of those around him. When other pastors fled for safety, he stayed on, eventually conducting more than 4,500 funeral services that year. One of those was for his wife.

And yet at some point amid these dire events, Martin composed a family grace to be said by his children before meals—a hymn still sung today all across Germany at state occasions and national days of remembrance:

"Now thank we all our God,
With hearts and hands and voices,
Who wondrous things hath done,
In whom His world rejoices;

Who from our mother's arms
Hath blessed us on our way
With countless gifts of love,
And still is ours today."

When we sing these words in the comfortable surroundings of a Thanksgiving service at church, we smell turkey in the oven, warm bread on the table. We hear the voices of relatives, enjoying reconnecting and conversing with one another. But make no mistake, this joy-filled refrain wasn't birthed in the settled quiet of a country cottage. It was forged in pain and suffering and grief and death. True thanksgiving comes at a cost. And no circumstances are so dire that they can't produce hymns of joy and thanks on the lips of those who know their God.

A Debt We Can Repay

"I must perform my vows to you, O God;
I will render thank offerings to you" (Psalm 56:12)

Have you ever been in a trial or extreme difficulty and vowed in the darkness, "Lord, if you get me out of this mess, I vow to thank you for it."? David was in that very predicament when he wrote Psalm 56. He was always getting into scrapes. If it wasn't self-induced, then it was probably coming from one of his many enemies. In this case the Philistines had captured him, and now he was a POW. "Deliver me from captivity, and I promise when I get out of here, I'll give you thanks for doing it!" The problem is when we do get out from underneath that burden, all of a sudden the birds are chirping, the sun is out, and there is a very rational explanation for the deliverance. And off we go with life—like the ten lepers Jesus healed, and only one returned to thank Him. I'm sure the other nine had very plausible reasons not to return and give thanks. Besides, I'm sure they now were very busy with their newfound lease on life.

And yet, gratitude is something we owe. It's a debt. When we bring our thanks before God, we are recognizing Him as the source of all that is good, *"for every good and perfect gift comes from above"* (James 1:17). If it's good, it's from Him. And because it's from Him, we owe Him both the courtesy and duty of saying simply, "thank you." So, remember this when it's Thanksgiving: You can consume 5000 calories and watch endless hours of football and still not experience Thanksgiving.

WINTER

No winter lasts forever;
no spring skips its turn.
Hal Borland

Rest

Let me (Steve) be brutally honest--I don't like WINTER. In the Seattle area, the days become very short, it seems there is no end to the gray, the temperatures are cold (ok, the days aren't Fargo cold), and my skin is getting thinner. And for all you youngsters out there, driving on a rainy night in the dark is quite an adventure for us older types. For safety reasons, I feel like there needs to be a moratorium for all pedestrians while I drive on one of those nights. So, call me a wimp, but I think I'm more suited for 73-degree weather 365 days a year, with night ceasing and beginning based on my own personal sleeping patterns.

Fortunately, we have a beautiful reprieve in WINTER: It's called Christmas. Perfectly placed in the darkest time of the year is the greatest and brightest Light the world has ever seen. How blessed and fortunate we are to live in our world, and not in C.S. Lewis's world of *Narnia*....at least when the White Witch was ruling. *"'It is winter in Narnia,' said Mr. Tumnus, 'and has been for ever so long...always winter, but never Christmas.'"* What a horrible plight that would be. Or imagine living under the evil reign of the Sheriff of Nottingham, played by Alan Rickman in *Robin Hood*, *"Cancel the kitchen scraps for lepers and orphans! No more merciful beheadings! And cancel Christmas!"* Yes, a WINTER without Christmas would surely be, in my mind, a season we could entirely skip over.

To the degree I do not like this particular season, is the degree to which I now love and embrace it in a metaphorical sense. Many years ago, my life was completely transformed by the reading of the book *Anonymous*, by *Alicia Britt Chole*. At the time I was wrestling with self-doubt regarding my own worth before God, in that the ministries I had been actively leading and involved in had come to an abrupt ending. I felt like the rug had been pulled out from underneath me, and I was now on God's spiritual bench. After struggling for many months, I came across her book and could not put it down. It was as though God was speaking directly through her writings to the WINTERY plight of my soul:

In winter, are the trees bare? Yes.

In winter, are the trees barren? No.

Life still is.

Life does not sleep – though in winter she retracts all advertisement. And when she does so, she is conserving and preparing for the future.

And so it is with us. Seasonally, we too are stripped of visible fruit. Our giftings are hidden; our abilities are underestimated. When previous successes fade and current efforts falter, we can easily mistake our fruitlessness for failure.

But such is the rhythm of spiritual life: new growth, fruitfulness, transition, rest. Abundance may make us feel more productive, but perhaps emptiness has greater power to strengthen our souls.

In spiritual winters, our fullness is thinned so that, undistracted by our giftings, we can focus upon our character. In the absence of anything to measure, we are left with nothing to stare at except for our foundation.

Risking inspection, we begin to examine the motivations that support our deeds, the attitudes that influence our words, the dead wood otherwise hidden beneath our busyness. Then a life-changing transition occurs as we move from resistance through repentance to the place of rest. With gratitude, we simply abide. Like a tree planted by living water, we focus upon our primary responsibility: remaining in Him.

In winter are we bare? Yes.

In winter are we barren? No.

True life still is.

The Father's work in us does not sleep – though in spiritual winters he retracts all advertisement. And when he does so, he is purifying our faith, strengthening our character, conserving our energy, and preparing us for the future.

The sleepy days of winter hide us so that the seductive days of summer will not ruin us.

What beautiful words to encourage the despondent soul living in apparent anonymity. Yes, God has so arranged our climate with four distinct seasons in order to help us better understand the seasons of life and of the soul. So, if you are currently in a season of WINTER, or soon will be, know it is a season of life we all so desperately need.

Waiting is the Catalyst

"From of old no one has heard or perceived by the ear, no eye has seen a God beside you, who acts for those who wait for him"
(Isaiah 64:4).

In this fast-paced world where we want everything now, waiting can be hard. Nothing tries our faith like waiting on God for answers to prayer. And to compound the dilemma of having to wait, we typically define it in a very *passive* sense. We say we're waiting for SUMMER to come, the school year to end, or a package to arrive. It's not something we're thinking about all the time. Only when something jogs our memory do we focus on it. But the word "wait" in Isaiah 64:4 is an *active* word. It means to long for, to cling or adhere to. It has the sense of something that is uppermost and at the forefront of a person's mind.

It is this kind of active waiting that generates action. Action not on the part of the one who is waiting, but upon the God they are waiting on. For He's there waiting to act for those who wait expectantly for Him. And therein lies the rub. If we run ahead of God, like Abraham did with Ishmael, our manipulation of circumstances, and the timing of them, will only lead us to turmoil, exhaustion, and failure. But on the other hand, if we wait attentively and expectantly for Him, Isaiah says in 64:5 He will *"meet"* with us. And that's called grace. The grace to wait on His purposes until the precise moment when He gives evidence He was working all along.

The Work of Waiting

"But let patience have its perfect work, that you may be perfect and complete, lacking nothing" (James 1:4).

Yesterday I drove State Route 26 that connects Vantage with Colfax. This two-lane highway was a test of my patience as I got behind slow moving RV's, farm machinery, and folks out for what must have been a leisurely Sunday drive. As I experienced a testing of my patience on that long highway, I was reminded of something I was told many years ago. *"If somebody says, 'I've been patiently waiting for you', then they've actually been very impatient."* Vehicles driving ten mph under the speed limit. Selecting the line at a grocery store in need of multiple price checks. The eternal wait in a physician waiting room. We've developed microwave expectations in a world seemingly moving at the speed of a glacier.

In addition to not being in vogue, patience also seems so passive and inactive. In a world valuing activity, performance, and Amazon same-day delivery, patiently waiting is not a sought-after societal virtue; however, when we wait on the Lord it's actually quite active. The activity isn't our own, but His. As we trust in His perfect timetable, He changes us from the inside out. Sure, we want what we want when we want it, but as we learn to take a deep breath and look to Him, He will slowly but surely quiet our souls and deposit this fruit of the Spirit in us.

"Wait on the Lord; be of good courage, and he shall strengthen your heart; wait, I say, on the Lord. Truly my soul silently waits for God; from Him comes my salvation" (Psalm 27:14; 62:1).

God's Math: 5 = 2

"His Lord said to him, 'Well done, good and faithful servant; you have been faithful over a few things, I will make you ruler over many things. Enter into the joy of your Lord'" (Matthew 25:21, 23).

In the Parable of the Talents found in Matthew 25, Jesus talks about three people. I'd like to focus on the first two, one who was given five talents, and the other who was given two. What I find fascinating in this parable is the reaction of the Lord to these two very different servants. Both were faithful, but one had received and produced much more than the other one. And yet, the Lord has exactly the same response to each servant (verses 21 and 23). In a very real way, we learn here in God's value system, five equals two. Unfortunately, our eyes are inclined to see things much differently. The prison of comparison will always leave us looking down in pride on the one with two, or feeling like a failure as we look up to the one with five.

But God's view of His children is so different than this. While those of us with "two talents" might think we *"only have five loaves and two fish"* (John 6:9) to offer, God says that's enough to feed five thousand. Or we might think our meager offerings are like the widow's mite, but Jesus says, *"this poor widow has put in more than all"* (Mark 12:43). This incongruency between how we calculate value and how God does should not surprise us, for He told us *"My thoughts are not your thoughts, neither are your ways my ways"* (Isaiah 55:8). God doesn't compare one child of His to another. So, let's start to see how God sees, and be set free from comparing ourselves to others. If you have been given "less" than others, you can be at peace with this apparent inequality. Do not diminish, devalue, or minimize your talents. For if you make it your life ambition to be faithful with whatever you have, He too will say of you, *"Well done, good and faithful servant.....enter into the joy of your Lord"* (Matthew 25:23).

Learning to Trust

"Some trust in chariots, and some in horses;
but we will trust in the name of the Lord our God" (Psalm 20:7).

I'm sure in the day, if we were involved in a war, we'd want a plethora of chariots and horses on our side. For like anything in life, we absolutely need physical things in order to survive and succeed. So, the issue is not the use of what we have at our disposal, but where our reliance is. As trust is at the core of human relationships, so trust is central to our relationship with God. He graciously *"gives us all things to enjoy"* (1 Timothy 6:17), such as money, family, friends, life insurance, clothing, food, shelter, etc.. To trust in those things is another matter. A life-long journey is the pursuit of finding that perfect harmony between the use of the creation and our trust in the Creator.

As Charles Spurgeon once stated,

> "Would we run so hastily to others for assistance if we remembered that the Lord is magnified by our implicit reliance upon His solitary arm? 'But', say one, 'aren't human resources to be used?' Certainly, but our fault seldom lies in their neglect. Far more frequently it springs out of foolishly believing in them instead of believing in God. Few neglect human resources, but many sin greatly in making too much of them."

Rest

"There remains therefore a rest for the people of God.
For he who has entered His rest has himself also ceased from his
works as God did from His" (Hebrews 4: 9-10).

I don't know about you, but when I get to the end of a long week, I really want to rest. What joy there is getting into bed at the close of the week and NOT setting my alarm clock. It seems like we're always battling fatigue in some form. Throw a few kids and animals into the mix and it exponentiates. Fortunately, we live in a city abounding in that over-the-counter stimulant called caffeine.

With so many demands in life, and so much work to be done, it's comforting to know with God you can find true rest for your soul. *"Come to Me, all of you who are weary and carry heavy burdens, and I will give you rest"* (Matthew 11:28). When Jesus said on the cross, *"It is finished"* (John 19:30), He declared the perfect work required by His Father had been fully completed. There's nothing more we can do—or need to do—to add to it. It is fully and completely finished. So then what are we to do? Believe! Too good to be true, we say. We must earn it and work for it like everything else in life. Well, that's the exact same mindset Jesus encountered 2000 years ago:

> *"'What shall we do that we may work the works of God?' Jesus answered and said to them, 'This is the work of God, that you believe in Him whom He sent'"* (John 6:28-29).

What funny creatures we are. Always dreaming of escapes from work and finding more rest in life, we come to God and want to work. Yet this is the source of joy, peace, and hope: Resting in the finished work of Jesus Christ and His unconditional love for you. *"For we who have believed do enter that rest"* (Hebrews 4:3).

The Woman at the Well

*"Come, see a Man who told me all things that I ever did.
Could this be the Christ?" (John 4:29).*

Marginalized by those who disdained her life choices, the Samaritan woman was relegated to collect water from Jacob's well in the heat of the day. Having had five husbands and now living with a man, she was an outcast, rejected by the religious and living on the fringes of the Samaritan city of Sychar. Adding insult to injury, not only did her fellow Samaritans reject her, but to the Jews she was a half-breed, a mixed ethnicity resulting from the Assyrian conquest centuries before.

And yet Jesus *"needed to go through Samaria"* (John 4:4). Why? All good Jews went around Samaria when traveling north and south. And if they, for some reason, had to go through, the last thing that would happen would be for a Jewish man to engage with a Samaritan woman in conversation. But Jesus needed to go through, because he needed to meet the one who was loved by His Father. The one who was dismissed, ridiculed, and rejected. The one whom humanity had cast aside, this was the very one the Father sent His Son to meet, for He loved her.

And He also loves you. With all your frailties, failures, and faults, if you were the only one, this same Jesus would abandon heaven and come to you too. Which in fact, He did. *"Suppose one of you had a hundred sheep and lost one. Wouldn't you leave the ninety-nine in the wilderness and go after the lost one until you found it?"* (Luke 15:4).

If Only

"....I have learned to be content whatever the circumstances. I know what it is to be in need, and I know what it is to have plenty. I have learned the secret of being content in any and every situation, whether well fed or hungry, whether living in plenty or in want. I can do everything through Christ who gives me strength"
(Philippians 4:11-13).

Contentment does not come naturally. You are not born being content, but instead we learn it (hopefully) over the course of a lifetime. Our desires for that which we do not possess are quite strong, for the temptation is to believe joyous living is in receiving that which we do not have. However true joy is not getting whatever we want, but learning how to gratefully receive what God has already given us. It is a lie to believe in the foolish realm of "if only." "If only I was married." If only I was *not* married." "If only we had children." "If only we did *not* have children." "If only it was warm outside." "If only I had more money." "If only (fill in the blank)"

The reality is, if we are not content with what we have, we will never be content with what we think we want. The key to joyous living is to embrace the will of God and to receive with gratitude the gifts He chooses to give us in each season of life. And as we draw closer and closer to Christ, we will find increasing sufficiency in Him, for we are told *"...we are complete in Him"* (Colossians 2:10). He truly is enough, as the author of Psalm 73:25 discovered, *"Whom do I have in heaven but you? And with you, I lack nothing on earth."*

Overloaded

*"Blessed be the Lord, who daily loads us with benefits,
the God of our salvation!" (Psalm 68:19).*

Many years ago, a good friend of ours with cancer began journaling in her darkest hour all the things she was thankful for. Today, now cancer-free, she continues daily in her gratitude journal and is now close to 25,000 entries.

Charles Spurgeon once said, *"Let us daily praise God for common mercies— common as we frequently call them, and yet so priceless that when deprived of them we are ready to perish."*

It is so easy to take these "common mercies" for granted, to be deceived in thinking every good and perfect gift has *not* come from above, but from Fred Meyer, Target, or Amazon. While it may be common to consider worship something constrained to fifteen minutes on a Sunday morning, in reality we've been designed to praise our Creator daily, seeing Him as the source of all these common mercies.

So, let's not walk past and miss the countless reasons for worship each and every day: pillows, blankets, and mattresses. Coffee and creamer. Hot water, shampoo, and toothbrushes. Paved roads, turn signals, and traffic lights. Chairs, carpet, tables, and ink pens. Warm clothes, blue skies, and Jolly Time Kettle Corn. There you go: 18 common mercies. I have 24,982 to go. For when Ephesians 5:20 encourages us towards *"giving thanks always and for everything to God the Father,"* this is not only possible, but can easily be achieved without repetition.

Mind Renewal

"And do not be conformed to this world, but be transformed by the renewing of your mind, that you may prove what is that good and acceptable and perfect will of God" (Romans 12:2).

In this odyssey we call life, one of the great existential questions all believers have asked on more than one occasion is, "What is God's will for my life?" It may be something small, or it could be life-altering. Romans 12:2 gives us a simple (but not easy) pathway to knowing God's will—renew your mind. But how? By reading the gift God gave us for that very thing—the Bible. Sure, there's been plenty of abuse and misuse of the Bible over the centuries, but the intention of God is that His living and active Word would be the means by which renewal would occur. So the question is not "Am I in the Word?", but "Is the Word in me?" For in Colossians 3:16, we're instructed to *"Let the word of Christ dwell in you richly…"*

As we meditate and believe on the promises, truths, and wisdom of the Bible, over time we begin to think the Bible vs. just read it. It becomes the prism by which we process and interpret reality, for emanating from the Bible we find our fundamental identify and purpose for living. And so, to the degree the Word is immersed in us, and believed by faith, is the degree to which our minds will be renewed.

Ephesians 6:17 says, *"Take…the sword of the Spirit, which is the Word of God."* This isn't some cute metaphorical language being used here. It is called a sword because we are actually supposed to kill something with it. We are to kill mindsets and strongholds based on lies like pessimism, victimhood, unworthiness, hopelessness, and fear. We are to fight and slay these lies with the truth. Just as Jesus defeated the devil's lies in Matthew 4, so can we. And as our minds renew (a lifelong process BTW), we too will be able to prove what is that good, acceptable, and perfect will of God.

The Price of Intimacy

*"...that you, being rooted and grounded in love, may be able
to comprehend with all the saints what is the width and length
and depth and height – to **know** the love of Christ which passes
knowledge; that you may be filled with all the fullness of God"
(Ephesians 3:17-19).*

The word "know" (*to know the love of Christ*) is not the same Greek word as "knowledge" *(which passes knowledge).* I've always been puzzled by this verse, as though we're being instructed to know something which cannot be known. This has always sounded like a complete exercise in futility to me. But that's not it at all. The word "know" here is referencing having a personal, first-hand experience of intimate love for—and with—Christ. That is what surpasses and is greater than "knowledge" (intellectual comprehension and awareness of information and facts). It's intimate love with Christ which surpasses head knowledge. It's also the same word used by Paul, when writing from a prison cell, he says, *"That I may know* (intimate love) *Him and the power of His resurrection and the fellowship of His sufferings, being conformed to His death"* (Philippians 3:10). Paul was so passionately desirous of greater intimacy with Christ, he desired sufferings and death so he might gain even deeper fellowship with Christ which only pain could bring. From a human perspective, that is completely incomprehensible!

True intimacy always carries with it a very high price to pay, for vulnerability will always expose us to the risk of much sorrow, anguish, and pain. But there is no other path on earth to wholeness and life with God and with those we love. Ultimately, that which will draw us closer to the love of Christ and to our neighbor is that which is good. Maybe not as the world defines good, but surely as God does.

Towards the Storm

"When you pass through the waters, I will be with you; and when you pass through the rivers, they will not sweep over you"
(Isaiah 43:2).

Recently my son shared a fact I was unaware of regarding the buffalo and cows that roam and graze near each other in Colorado. While similar in many ways, how they react to WINTER storms is quite different. When storms approach from the west, cows will scatter in fear to the east, believing they can outrun the storm and avoid it. Their response only keeps them in the storm longer, extending their pain and discomfort. Buffaloes, on the other hand, come together as a herd and run straight into the storm. By moving towards it in unity, they actually shorten the time spent in it and reduce the storm's negative impact.

Just like with weather, the storms of life are inevitable. What isn't inevitable is how we choose to deal with the storm. Will we confidently face the storm with faith that God is with us, and His promises are just as true in the darkness as they were in the light? Or will we scatter and attempt to flee that which has been dialed up for us? Will we weather the storm and emerge on the other side closer to God? Or will we be beaten up by it, worn out and bitter? While the flight response of the amygdala is real, God's grace is greater. He is with you, and He *"will never leave you nor forsake you"* (Deuteronomy 31:8). So do not fear the storms of life. Use the storms to become stronger, trusting Him more and drawing closer to those around you.

In The Dark

"Do not rejoice over me, my enemy; when I fall, I will arise;
when I sit in darkness, the Lord will be my light" (Micah 7:8).

All around us, life and beauty spring from darkness. In the old days, a photographer knew, in order to achieve a beautiful picture, the film would need time to develop in the dark. A seed, if it is going to blossom into a beautiful flower, must first be buried in the dirt. Before it reveals its glory in the light, it must first be hidden in the darkness of the earth. A baby requires nine months in the pitch-black arena of their mother's womb before ever seeing the brightness of day. The trees around us seem so bare in the darkness of Winter, and yet we know they are not barren for Spring is about to arrive. And even with all we know about Jesus, 90% of his life on earth has been hidden from our sight.

God has ordered His world in such a way that darkness frequently precedes light. Winter always precedes Spring. For death must occur before there is any resurrection. We can be confident knowing when we are in the dark, He is not. For the Lord is like a skilled photographer, knowing exactly how long it will take for beauty and purpose to develop. When the time is right (His time, not ours), He will walk in and turn on the light, revealing your story and His beautiful picture displaying hope to a hurting world. Jesus came to earth to do this very thing, *"To console those who mourn in Zion, to give them beauty for ashes, the oil of joy for mourning, the garment of praise for the spirit of heaviness"* (Isaiah 61:3).

When did we see you?

"Assuredly, I say to you, inasmuch as you did it to one of the least of these My brethren, you did it to Me" (Matthew 25:40).

Papa Panov's Special Christmas is a wonderful Christmas story written by Ruben Saillens and translated into English by Leo Tolstoy. In this short story, Papa Panov's Christmas wish was to worship the Christ Child and give Him the finest pair of shoes he's ever made. In a dream on Christmas Eve, he's promised that his wish will come true, but he must watch carefully for Jesus. And so, on Christmas day, Papa Panov eagerly waited for his Messiah to arrive. And arrive He did: the cold street sweeper he refreshed with a cup of hot coffee, the unemployed girl with a baby he outfitted with special shoes, and the beggars he fed out of his own supply of soup and bread. And yet, Papa Panov kept running to his window looking for this special visitor, anxious that he may have missed Him. Weary and tired by day's end, Papa Panov concluded it must have been just a dream after all. Jesus had not come. But then he had a vision, and in it Jesus Himself said, "I came to you today in every one of those you helped and welcomed." To where Papa Panov could joyfully conclude, "So He did come after all!"

In many ways we can be like Papa Panov, regularly running up to the window of our own life looking for Jesus, anxious that we too may have missed Him. But we haven't. Jesus just doesn't show up the way we would expect Him to, does He? A homeless couple in Bethlehem giving birth to a child in a barn surrounded by livestock. Who could have predicted that's how God would show up on this earth? And so, Christmas, and this story from Tolstoy, teach us an important principle of life: The most important person in the world is the person right in front of you.

How to Have a Wonderful Life

"And remember the words of the Lord Jesus, that He said,
'It is more blessed to give than to receive" (Acts 20:35).

I'm pretty certain none of us will ever have the life-altering experience of George Bailey, who was assisted by the angel Clarence to see what life would have been like without him. Wanting to see the world, he was supposedly trapped in boring old Bedford Falls trying to keep his father's "two-bit savings and loan" afloat. While his brother and friends rode off into the world to acquire fame and fortune, he was left behind to live out what seemed to be a mundane life in complete anonymity. And yet, seen through a different lens, his life of obscurity was anything but that.

In one scene in the movie, there's a framed saying under his father's picture. It says, *"All you can take with you is that which you've given away."* This one quote I believe encapsulates not only the essence of the movie, but also of life. Serving and sacrificing for others is the pathway to true riches. Unlike the greedy robber baron Mr. Potter, who saw material gain as the chief end of man, Jesus Christ showed us a different way to live and experience the *"abundant life."* So be assured your daily service and sacrifice for others is seen and recorded by your Heavenly Father. Your life matters, and one day soon, on the other side, you'll see just how significant it was. It's why Harry Bailey at the end of the movie raised a glass to George and said, "A toast to my big brother George: The richest man in town!"

On Pride and Humility

*"A proud man is always looking down on things and people:
and, of course, as long as you are looking down,
you cannot see something that is above you." C. S. Lewis*

*"Do not imagine that if you meet a really humble man he will be
what most people call 'humble' nowadays: he will not be a sort...
who is always telling you that, of course, he is a nobody. Probably
all you will think about him is that he seemed a cheerful, intelligent
chap who took a real interest in what you said to him. He will not be
thinking about humility: he will not be thinking about himself at all."*
C. S. Lewis

"God resists the proud, but gives grace to the humble" (1 Peter 5:5).

In Jesus we see the essence of perfect humility in bodily form. God stooping to become human, He was born in a feeding trough so He might one day die as a common criminal on a Roman cross. He came not to be served, but to serve. With our new identity as His adopted children, we too have been empowered to serve as we have been served.

Like Jesus, knowing our identity equips us for humble service of others:

"Jesus, knowing that the Father had given all things into His hands, and that He had come from God and was going to God, rose from supper... and began to wash the disciples' feet" (John 13:3).

Our Humble God

*"Let this mind be in you which was also in Christ Jesus...
being found in appearance as a man, He humbled Himself
and became obedient to the point of death" (Philippians 2:5,8).*

For many of us, *humble* is not an attribute we immediately ascribe to our triune God. And yet, *"Who is like the Lord our God, who dwells on high, who humbles Himself to behold the things that are in the heavens and in the earth?"* (Psalm 113:5-6). Or Jesus as he describes Himself, *"Take My yoke upon you and learn from Me, for I am gentle and humble in heart, and you will find rest for your souls"* (Matthew 11:29). And one of the fruits of the Holy Spirit in Galatians is *"...humility (gentleness)."* Our infinite, eternal, omnipotent, omniscient, omnipresent God is humble. What He asks us to be, He already is.

C. S. Lewis said, *"Humility isn't thinking less about yourself, it's thinking about yourself less."* An outward, other-centered orientation. The antithesis of pride. For the Christian, the road to growing humility begins with a comprehension of our new identify in Christ. *"I have been crucified with Christ; it is no longer I who live, but Christ lives in me"* (Galatians 2:20). Christ in you (the One *humble in heart*), is the new you. Adopted, accepted, loved, and redeemed, you are a new creation in Christ. Knowing the real you enables you to serve and love others (see John 13:3-5). And then, as we grow in setting our attention and affections away from ourselves and on Christ in prayer, worship, and reading His Word, the lifetime process of thinking of ourselves less gradually gains traction, discovering JOY in its rightful order:

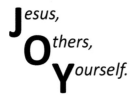

J*esus,*
O*thers,*
Y*ourself.*

The Light of the World

"Then Jesus spoke to them again, saying,
"I am the light of the world. He who follows Me
shall not walk in darkness, but have the light of life" (John 8:12).

We live in a very dark world. We need light. We need physical light, for December is our darkest month. And we need spiritual light, for spiritual darkness abounds. We need Christmas! And this is why Jesus came into the world, to extinguish all that is dark. For John said,

> *"In Him was life, and that life was the light of all mankind. The light shines in the darkness, and the darkness has not overcome it"* (John 1:4-5).

A few verses later, John goes on to say Jesus *"was the true Light which gives light to every man coming into the world"* (v. 9). Yes, walking in the light as He is in the Light (as opposed to walking in darkness) is the path to true freedom, authenticity, and joy. For Jesus said, *"I have come that they may have life, and that they may have it more abundantly"* (John 10:10). He came to die, so we might live. So now we can sing:

> *Joy to the world, the Lord is come*
> *Let earth receive her King*
> *Let every heart prepare Him room*
> *And Heaven and nature sing*
> *And Heaven and nature sing*
> *And Heaven, and Heaven, and nature sing*

Sight for the Blind

"The people who walk in darkness will see a great light. For those who live in a land of deep darkness, a light will shine" (Isaiah 9:2).

Tilted at twenty-three degrees so we can enjoy our four seasons, the earth hurtles at nineteen miles per second through space in an orbit around the sun, traveling 600 million miles a year. Contemplating humanity and the cosmos in which we reside, the American astronomer and astrophysicist Carl Sagan concluded,

> "Our planet is a lonely speck in the great enveloping cosmic dark. In our obscurity, in all this vastness, there is no hint that help will come from elsewhere to save us from ourselves."

Talk about hopelessness. "Lonely speck… cosmic dark… obscurity… no hint that help will come." Well Mr. Sagan, I fortunately have some good news for you: God has sent us His hint, from a dimension you never saw through your many telescopes. While we do indeed live on a lonely speck, we are not alone. For we have seen a great Light, and His name is Jesus. He is that very help we needed to save us from ourselves. Born to die, Jesus became our light, enabling those who once groped in darkness to see. As John Newton wrote in Amazing Grace, *"I once was lost, but now I'm found, was blind but now I see."* This is the hope and joy of Christmas, for the light has shone, and the deep darkness is no more.

Outside In

"'Behold, the virgin shall be with child, and bear a Son, and they shall call His name Immanuel,' which is translated, 'God with us'"
(Matthew 1:23).

Christmas is about God coming to us. Imprisoned behind bars that can only be opened from the outside, God sends God, and the Giver becomes the Gift. This baby in a manger is the long-awaited key sent to swing wide the locked doors of our souls and set us free. *"So if the Son sets you free, you will be free indeed"* (John 8:36). Unlike religious performance where humanity attempts to come to God, Christ comes and says, "Let Me do the work." This is why He could boldly say, *"I always do those things that please my Father"* (John 8:29), and *"It is finished"* (John 19:30) when He was on the cross, for He is our full and complete performance. We cannot add to or detract from Christ, for *"It is finished"*. His performance has received His Father's full and complete satisfaction. This is the good news of Christmas. The gift of Christmas. The joy of Christmas. The prison doors have swung wide open, so come out you captives, believe and be free!

Dietrich Bonhoeffer, imprisoned for his faith, said the following,

"A prison cell, in which one waits, hopes... and is completely dependent on the fact that the door of freedom has to be opened from the outside, is not a bad picture of Advent."

So, in this season of Advent, let's be singing:

Come, Thou long expected Jesus
Born to set Thy people free;
From our fears and sins release us,
Let us find our rest in Thee.
Israel's strength and consolation,
Hope of all the earth thou art;
Dear desire of every nation,
Joy of every longing heart.

The Prince of Peace

"For unto us a Child is born, unto us a Son is given;
and the government will be upon His shoulder.
And His name will be called Wonderful Counselor, Mighty God,
Everlasting Father, Prince of Peace" (Isaiah 9:6).

While many of us may have the latest iPhone on our Christmas wish list, many more of us have Christmas lists with longings more like these: a broken heart mended, reconciliation of a severed relationship, to be cancer-free, to see a wayward child return home, or to see an end to all the bickering at home. In other words, we long for peace. In a world full of conflict, where polarization, loneliness, and anxiety have reached unprecedented levels in our digitally connected world, Christmas calls us to turn away from all this noise and look up to the One who alone is our Peace.

> *"Peace I leave with you; my peace I give to you. Not as the world gives do I give to you. Let not your hearts be troubled, neither let them be afraid"* (John 14:27).

The cross of Christ was the bridge God provided to lead us back to peace with Him. When we surrender to Him, and have peace *with* God, we then are enabled to experience the peace *of* God. Only in Christ—the Prince of Peace— can we know the peace that replaces disagreement with unity, turmoil with calm, strife with harmony, restlessness with contentment, angst with joy. *"... and the peace of God, which surpasses all understanding, will guard your hearts and* minds *through Christ Jesus"* (Philippians 4:7).

Wonderful Counselor

"To us a child is born, to us a son is given,
and the government shall be on his shoulder,
and his name shall be called Wonderful Counselor, Mighty God,
Everlasting Father, Prince of Peace" (Isaiah 9:6).

How difficult it is when someone divulges and reveals to us their many deep wounds, traumatic events, abusive relationships, and childhood scars. It's burdensome to know what counsel to give to help them in their healing journey. I'm not a professional counselor, so I can only imagine how overwhelming this must be for those called daily to serve those in such profound pain.

Whether you provide counsel for a living or do it as a natural function of your daily life, it's so reassuring to know we have a Wonderful Counselor to help us. Pressing into Him, we can trust He will provide just the right words at just the right time. Literally translated *"a wonder of a counselor,"* you can rest assured He is the ultimate fountain of all wisdom, knowledge, and understanding. Draw near to Him, and He will draw near to you.

> *"If any of you lack wisdom, let him ask of God, who gives to all liberally and without reproach, and it will be given to him" (James 1:5).*

> *"… the sheep hear His voice; and He calls his own sheep by name… He goes before them; and the sheep follow Him, for they know His voice" (John 10:3-4).*

> *"Whether you turn to the right or to the left, your ears will hear a voice behind you, saying, "This is the way; walk in it" (Isaiah 30:21).*

> *"…do not worry about how or what you should speak. For it will be given to you in that hour what you should speak; for it is not you who speak, but the Spirit of your Father who speaks in you" (Matt. 10:19-20).*

Awe and Wonder

"And she brought forth her firstborn Son, and wrapped Him in swaddling clothes, and laid Him in a manger, because there was no room for them in the inn" (Luke 2:7).

There are many forces in life that make us numb to the miraculous and breathtaking. The oft repeated story becomes familiar, and as the saying goes, "familiarity breeds contempt." Self-sufficiency can also rob us of the joyful expectation this season affords. Why look for a Savior when we can do it ourselves? And of course, the busyness of this time of year. Who has time? We still have presents to buy and meals to prepare. And after seeing a plethora of CGI generated movies in our digitized age, haven't we seen it all? What in this boring world could possibly top that? Oh, how easy it is to be in awe of the work of our own hands.

Fighting against these forces, we need to regain our sense of what real awe and wonder might actually look like. Seeing Christmas through the eyes of a little child is one simple litmus test to evaluate just how jaded we may have become. For Jesus said, *"I tell you the truth, unless you change and become like little children, you will never enter the kingdom of heaven."* (Matthew 18:3), and *"From the lips of children and infants you, Lord, have called forth your praise"* (Matthew 21:16). Seen through those eyes, what is more miraculous than the impossibility of God coming to us?

A holy God made a way for all who believe to come to Him... by first coming to us. *"We love because He first loved us"* (1 John 4:19). So this season, ask God to fill you again with wonder. For God has stooped to come to earth, a virgin is about to give birth, and angelic choirs will light up the dark Bethlehem sky. Let's recover the shock of who this baby was and why He was born, holding in reverence the One who alone is to be held in such awe and wonder.

A Charlie Brown Christmas

"For God so loved the world that He gave His only begotten Son, that whoever believes in Him should not perish but have everlasting life"
(John 3:16).

On Thursday December 9, 1965, at 7:30 pm (pre-empting The Munsters), CBS premiered the animated special *"A Charlie Brown Christmas"*. CBS executives thought it would be a dismal flop due to its quirky animation, slow pace, absence of a laugh track, use of jazz music, and having actual children to do the voice overs vs. trained voice actors (several of the voices coming from children who lived in the producer's neighborhood). But with Coca-Cola having commissioned and sponsored the special, the network decided to put it out there one time, expecting a ratings disaster. Needless to say, it was not.

In the show, Charlie Brown asks Linus Van Pelt a very profound question, "Isn't there anyone who knows what Christmas is all about?" Linus responds,

> "Sure, Charlie Brown, I can tell you what Christmas is all about. 'And there were in the same country shepherds abiding in the field, keeping watch over their flock by night. And lo, the angel of the Lord came upon them, and the glory of the Lord shone round them: and they were sore afraid. And the angel said unto them, 'Fear not: For behold, I bring unto you good tidings of great joy, which shall be to all people. For unto you is born this day in the city of David a Savior, which is Christ the Lord. And this shall be a sign unto you; Ye shall find the babe wrapped in swaddling clothes, lying in a manger.' And suddenly there was with the angel a multitude of the heavenly host, praising God, and saying, 'Glory to God in the highest, and on earth peace, good will toward men.'"

"That's what Christmas is all about, Charlie Brown."

A Lamb Without Blemish

*"And this will be the sign to you: You will find a Babe
wrapped in swaddling clothes, lying in a manger" (Luke 2:12).*

Who were the *"shepherds living out in the fields, keeping watch over their
flock by night"* (Luke 2:8)? These were not normal shepherds. They were
Levitical Shepherds, chosen and trained to attend the flock of sheep used as
sacrificial lambs in the Temple, especially at the time of Passover. Sacrificial
lambs had to be "spotless and without blemish." When a mother ewe was
about to give birth, she was taken to a cave designated for the birth of
sacrificial lambs. This cave was kept sterile and clean for the arrival of newborn
sacrificial lambs. Upon birth, the newborn lamb was immediately wrapped
in clean swaddling clothes to protect and keep it from blemish and danger.
Then the lamb would be placed in a stone feeding trough—a manger—until
a priest came to inspect it and declare it without blemish.

Many years later, John the Baptist *"saw Jesus coming toward him and said,
'Look, the Lamb of God, who takes away the sin of the world"* (John 1:29). And
Paul would refer to Jesus as *"our Passover Lamb"* (I Corinthians 5:7). From
the very beginning of His life, Jesus was presented to the world as the Lamb
of God, born to take away the sins of the world. This then is Christmas: God
becoming man, living a sinless life to die on the cross to pay the penalty for
our sins. The great exchange: His life for ours.

Gifts Fit for a King

"They entered the house and saw the child with his mother, Mary,
and they bowed down and worshiped him.
Then they opened their treasure chests and gave him gifts of gold,
frankincense, and myrrh" (Matthew 2:11).

Contrary to popular depictions, the wise men (or Magi) did not visit the baby Jesus in the manger but came to Him as a toddler living in His home in Nazareth. Magi, in that time period, had tremendous influence, and were a combination of scientists, politicians, and religious leaders. There really is nothing comparable in our western culture. And we don't really know how many there were of them. We just know there were three kinds of gifts. In that time, when heads of state arrived to visit a king, they came bearing many gifts. Gold was a gift for a king; frankincense was rare and so valuable it could be more expensive than gold and was predominantly connected with the priesthood. And myrrh, an aromatic substance produced from exotic trees in Eastern lands, symbolically prophesied Christ's death.

Imagine: A huge caravan of soldiers, bodyguards, and animals carrying immense treasure, going through the streets of Jerusalem saying over and over again, "Where is the King of the Jews? Where is He? Have you seen Him?" No wonder the tyrant Herod was so paranoid that his throne would soon be stolen by this toddler king. So, what can we learn from the Magi? We learn these mighty men would not stop until they found Jesus. They were tenacious in their search for the King of Kings and the Lord of Lords. And when they did find him, they did what was only appropriate—they bowed down and worshipped their King and their Lord. So, like those great gift givers of old, let's worship our King and not lose our wonder this season.

Where are you?

"When the cool evening breezes were blowing, the man and his wife heard the Lord God walking about in the garden. So they hid from the Lord God among the trees. Then the Lord God called to the man, 'Where are you?'" (Genesis 3:8-9).

When you wander, God comes looking for you. And when you are lost, as Adam and Eve were, the first question one must ask is *Where am I?* Ann Voskamp said, *"Our fall was, has always been, and always will be, that we aren't satisfied in God and what He gives. We hunger for something more, something other."* And yet none of our trivial pursuits will ever satisfy. And so, the first question God asks man in the Old Testament is relational, showing initiation in reaching out to him. And we see the first question in the New Testament being asked by men who wanted to know the whereabouts of their God and King, *"Where is He?"* (Matthew 2:2), for wise men are only wise because they make their chief purpose the seeking of Christ.

While the one common theme in all humanity's religions is man reaching after God, yet in all His relationships, we see God reaching for man. He reaches for you when your heart is broken, when shame bears down upon you, and when pain is covered up by the thin veneer of a smiling façade. Your God refuses to give up on you. He looks for you when you've been betrayed by a friend, abandoned by those closest to you, and even when you think He Himself has forsaken you. Yes, in all three experiences He comes looking for you, for He Himself experienced the same between the Garden of Gethsemane and His death. In the end, this pursuit of you is the story of Christmas: *"Behold, the virgin shall be with child, and bear a Son, and they shall call His name Immanuel, which is translated, 'God with us'"* (Matthew 1:23).

Christmas is for Singing

"Oh, sing to the Lord a new song! Sing to the Lord, all the earth.
Sing to the Lord, bless His name; proclaim the good news
of His salvation from day to day" Psalm 96:1-2.

Adapted from *The Quiet Place*, a devotional by Nancy DeMoss Wolgemuth

Of all the songs contained in Scripture, it's fascinating to see how many are compressed into the beginning of Luke's gospel. And they are definitely not of the *Jingle Bells* and *Deck the Halls* genre. These songs seek to encapsulate God's glorious plan for redemption and salvation, His greatness and His goodness. They reverberate with wonder at the coming of our Lord and Savior to a Bethlehem manger. There is Elizabeth's song (1:42-45), Mary's song... or the *Magnificat* (1:46-55), Zechariah's song (1:68-79), the angel's announcement (2:10-12), followed by the *Gloria* of the angel chorus (2:14), concluding with Simeon's song of worship to the child Jesus in the Temple (2:29-32).

So if you find the busyness of your holiday season exhausting and wearisome, or if this time of year conjures up for you feelings of sadness or loss, maybe it would be life for your soul to spend some time joining the angels and those who have gone before... and sing. Elevate your soul from the pressing matters at hand, and experience yet again the joy of this particular season. It is unlike any other, so I encourage you to read those first two chapters of Luke with fresh eyes and be transported back in time, and to your first love. And then sing!

> *Hark! the herald angels sing*
> *"Glory to the newborn King!"*
> *Peace on earth, and mercy mild*
> *God and sinners reconciled."*
> *Joyful, all ye nations, rise*
> *Join the triumph of the skies;*
> *With th' angelic host proclaim*
> *"Christ is born in Bethlehem."*
> *Hark! the herald angels sing*
> *"Glory to the newborn King!"*

Christmas is for Singing (Part 2)

"Christ Jesus...made Himself of no reputation...and coming in the
likeness of men. And being found in appearance as a man,
He humbled Himself and became obedient to the point of death,
even the death of the cross" (Philippians 2:5-8).

Speaking of Christmas and songs, here are the lyrics of a favorite contemporary Christmas song of mine from the band *Downhere:*

Follow the star to a place unexpected,
would you believe, after all we've projected,
a Child in a manger?
Lowly and small, the weakest of all.
Unlikeliness hero, wrapped in his mother's shawl.
Just a child, is this who we've waited for?

Bringing our gifts for the newborn Savior.
All that we have, whether costly or meek
because we believe.
God for His honor, and frankincense for His pleasure,
and myrrh for the cross He will suffer.
Do you believe? Is this who we've waited for?

Because how many kings step down from their thrones,
how many Lords have abandoned their homes?
How many greats have become the least for me?
And how many gods have poured out their hearts
to romance a world that is torn all apart?
How many fathers gave up their sons for me?

Only One did that for me.

It is Well Even When it is Not

"Then Herod, when he saw that he was deceived by the wise men, was exceedingly angry; and he sent forth and put to death all the male children who were in Bethlehem and in all its districts, from two years old and under, according to the time which he had determined from the wise men" (Matthew 2:16).

As many people look forward to the Christmas season with great joy, wishing time would stop, there are just as many who wish it would pass ever so quickly because it is just too painful. Like Mary, Joseph, the angels, shepherds, and wise men who would forever recall that holy night in worshipful remembrance, there were many other families in that same vicinity who would painfully remember the horrific night when their sons were massacred by Herod. Great hope and great pain, all in the same story.

While many stories have happy endings, many more don't. Despite praying, hoping, dreaming, and even begging God for a miracle, life circumstances have turned out differently than expected. Regardless of what this season may hold for you, may you find your resting place in God. Honest with Him about the pain, grief, and struggle within your soul. He is your hope. You may not understand what He is up to, and He may never answer your question of "Why?", but this Christmas season may you position yourself to receive the abundant grace of God, the hope of the manger found in the person of Jesus Christ, our Prince of Peace.

From the hymn, *It is Well With My Soul:*

"Though Satan should buffet,
though trials should come.
Let this blessed assurance control,
that Christ has regarded my helpless estate
and hath shed His own blood for my soul.

It is well with my soul"

Be Sure To Put Your Coat On

"The Spirit of the Lord God is upon Me (Jesus)...
He has sent Me to heal the brokenhearted... to console those who
mourn in Zion, to give them beauty for ashes,
the oil of joy for mourning, the garment of praise
for the spirit of heaviness" (Isaiah 61:1,3).

One of my favorite Christmas presents this year was a heated vest. I'm finding with age as my metabolism slows, fat layers disappear (in all the wrong places), and blood vessels lose their elasticity, my love for heat in these cold WINTER months is growing by the day. I may not be able to change the weather, but I can change my response to it.

In the same way, Isaiah says praise and worship works like a coat. When you put on a coat and it's cold, windy, and rainy outside, does the coat change the weather of the day? It doesn't change anything about the weather, does it? It changes you, in the weather. Praise and worship of Jesus is the way you clothe yourself for a very discouraging world. When we praise God in the midst of the stormy weather, we make a conscious and deliberate choice to change our focus, to push aside the things that may be worrying and discouraging us, and instead choose to focus on Him and His sovereignty, putting Him back on the throne of our life. We may not have any idea how it's all going to work out, but when we elevate Jesus, the very same stormy conditions and circumstances that were crushing us yesterday, we can thrive in today. And like Isaiah, we too can say,

> *"I will greatly rejoice in the Lord, My soul shall be joyful in my God; for He has clothed me with the garments of salvation, He has covered me with the robe of righteousness"* (Isaiah 61:10).

Quiet Spaces in the New Year

"And rising very early in the morning, while it was dark, He departed and went out to a desolate place, and there he prayed" (Mark 1:35).

We live in probably the noisiest time in the history of the world. While all generations have experienced the noise of children, machinery, the workplace, and the chattering of people, more recent analog generations have been able to layer on the additional noise emitting from radios, televisions, and stereos. But our generation takes the cake. In addition to all the rest, we get phones chirping and buzzing, emails, text messages, and IM's chiming, appliances dinging, vehicles warning, playlists playing, and video games making every conceivable noise. It seems we are surrounded 24/7 by sound and distraction. Our digital world produces a cacophony of sound. And if that weren't enough, we all must contend with the inner racket reverberating within our minds, which is perhaps the hardest realm of all to find a quiet space.

In this the new year, I encourage you to find daily quiet spaces to be alone with Jesus. In the quiet of the morning, day, or night, we all need to commune with Him and His love for us. Jesus said, *"If anyone thirsts, let him come to me and drink"* (John 7:37). Let us be thirsty souls for Him this year. But a word to the wise: Let your discipline always be less than your desire. Time with Him ought not to become a dutiful obligation, but a well of living water for those who thirst for a love only He can quench. So, this year, let us not become tyrannized by the urgent, allowing other sounds and voices to crowd out His voice. The path away from weariness and fatigue is not a digital escape, but it's to Him.

"The Lord is my shepherd; I shall not want. He makes me to lie down in green pastures; He leads me beside the still waters, He restores my soul" (Psalm 23:1-3).

Words of Life in the New Year

"So shall My word be that goes forth from My mouth; it shall not return void, but it shall accomplish what I please, and it shall prosper in the thing for which I sent it" (Isaiah 55:11).

The Bible is no ordinary book. While all other printed words are just that, words on a page, the Word of God *"is living and powerful,.....and is a discerner of the thoughts and intents of the heart"* (Hebrews 4:12) for *"all Scripture is given by inspiration of God"* (2 Timothy 3:16). Even Jesus, the incarnate Son of God, did not lean on His own understanding when confronted by the devil during His temptation in the wilderness. Instead, every time He was tempted by the enemy, He always quoted the Bible back to him, stating *"Man shall not live by bread alone, but by every word that proceeds from the mouth of God"* (Matthew 4:4). Jesus saw the Word of God as necessary to us as the food we eat daily to in order to survive.

Unfortunately, in our lifetime we are seeing the Bible relegated to just another app found amongst the two million in the App Store. George Gallup once said, "Americans revere the Bible, but by and large they don't read it. And because they don't read it, they have become a nation of biblical illiterates." A recent Barna poll found 12% of adults believed Joan of Arc was Noah's wife, 50% of graduating seniors thought Sodom and Gomorrah were a husband-and-wife team, and another poll had a considerable number of respondents indicating Billy Graham preached the sermon on the mount.

Please join me in praying for a greater hunger for God and His Word this upcoming year. Read and pray over Psalm 119, and may it become our reality in the new year:

"I have rejoiced in the way of your testimonies, as much as in all riches. I will delight myself in your statues; I will not forget your word. And I will delight myself in Your commandments, which I love. This is my comfort in my afflictions, for Your word has given me life. How sweet are Your words to my taste, sweeter than honey to my mouth! Your word is a lamp to my feet and a light to my path. I rejoice at Your word as one who finds great treasure."

The End Game

"We also glory in tribulations, knowing that tribulation produces perseverance; and perseverance, character; and character, hope"
(Romans 5:3-4).

The above passage gives us a pathway for Christian maturity. First, we learn to "glory" (rejoice) in the trials of life. Second, we persevere in this rejoicing. Third, we grow in Christian character (making good decisions). Now, one might think character would be the ultimate goal in the Christian life, but in fact, it is not. Our goal is ultimately hope (the confident expectation that good is coming). Our destination is not good actions, but a way of thinking called hope. For the kingdom of God moves forward primarily by what we believe, not by what we do. And hope is the soil that enables us to flourish in this life as we look forward to the next.

If you are one who seeks to export hope to others in the upcoming new year, it's imperative you regularly import hope for yourself. We do this by reading the promises in the Bible and taking God at His word, believing He is willing and able to do that which He has promised. For instance, when Moses sent the twelve spies into the promised land in Numbers 13, the spies were divided into two categories. These two groups saw the exact same circumstance (giants in the land!), but one group said they could be overcome, while the other group said they could not. One group had believing hope, while the other was afraid with unbelief. One group saw their big God, while the other group saw their big problem. So, let's be like the first group, praying the following for ourselves and others, *"Now may the God of hope fill you with all joy and peace in believing, that you may abound in hope by the power of the Holy Spirit"* (Romans 15:13).

But I Like The Way It Is

"Do not remember the former things, nor consider the things of old. Behold, I will do a new thing" (Isaiah 43:18-19).

I learned something new this week. When a mother eagle builds her nest, she starts by layering the nest with thorns, rocks, branches, and other sharp materials. Once that base is finished, she then provides a soft padding of feathers, fur, wool, and pine straw for her baby chicks. Eventually, when the eaglets are ready to fly, the mother eagle begins stirring up the nest, bringing up the thorns and sharp rocks to the surface, while slowly removing the comfortable feathers and other soft materials. In a deliberate process, the mother makes it very uncomfortable for her brood, prompting her children towards maturity, growth, and development outside the nest. Had the eaglets not been pushed out of their comfort zone, they would have never learned how to soar above the storms.

Change is never easy. And in this new year we'll probably experience plenty of it. Change appears to be the only constant in life (Can't I just keep my iPhone 7?). And yet God, it seems, is always prompting us to leave the nest. For our own good. For our own growth and development. Not prematurely, for that would be cruel. Instead, He promises upon leaving the nest, *"The eternal God is your refuge, and underneath are His everlasting arms"* (Deuteronomy 33:27). No matter how far we might fall during transition and change, He is always underneath. For His promise is always, *"I will never leave you nor forsake you"* (Deuteronomy 31:8). So, embrace change, risk, and challenge in your life. The discomfort you are feeling is frequently a prompting from God moving you forward to that which is good for you, in contrast to our proclivity to clutch on to that which is familiar.

Blue Monday?

"This is the day the Lord has made; we will rejoice and be glad in it"
(Psalm 118:24).

In 2005, a UK travel company by the name of Sky Travel issued a press release declaring the third Monday in January to be the most depressing day of the year. They even gave it the name *Blue Monday*. Supposedly built upon the research and calculations of psychologist Cliff Arnall, this specific day was deemed the saddest of the year due to a combination of factors: The fun and festivity of Christmas has become a distant memory, credit card statements have started rolling in revealing the financial damage of December, waistlines have magically expanded, new year's resolutions are falling to the wayside, there's not another paid holiday for months, the days are short, the nights are long, and weather has its icy grip on us. While the notion of one particular day being the saddest of them all has been debunked as a mere marketing ploy, January can still be a little gloomy.

Living in the cold dark days of January, it's reassuring to know the Lord is not constrained by the Gregorian calendar as we are. *"He is the same yesterday, today, and forever"* (Hebrews 13:8). His love for you never changes, and *"in His presence is fullness of joy"* (Psalm 16:11). For when we spend time in His presence, we find *"the joy of the Lord is our strength"* (Nehemiah 8:10).

So should you find yourself with that joyful strength today, please use it to build up those who might be down and need an encouraging word:

> *"Let us think of ways to motivate one another to acts of love and good works. And let us not neglect our meeting together, as some people do, but encourage one another, especially now that the day of His return is drawing near"* (Hebrews 10:24-25).

This day, and every day like it, is a day we can receive the joy of Jesus and shine His light to others.

Our Promised Land

"All these toys were never intended to possess my heart. My true good is in another world, and my only real treasure is Christ."
The Problem of Pain C. S. Lewis

"What does not satisfy when we find it, was not the thing we were desiring." The Pilgrim's Regress **C. S. Lewis**

"Whom have I in heaven but You? And there is none upon earth that I desire besides You" (Psalm 73:25).

What makes heaven... heaven? Is it heaven because there will be no more sin or evil of any kind? Is it where we'll be eternally healed and whole, never suffering again from the disease and death that plagued our lives here? Is heaven where grief and misery cease, where every tear is wiped away and unspeakable joy reigns forever? Or is it heaven because at last, we'll be reunited with all those we've loved and lost, never to be separated ever again?

These, and infinitely more, are the experiences followers of Christ will have as soon as we cross over death and into our promised land. And yet, while all these wonderful things do await us on the other side, it is not these that will satisfy our deepest longings. For heaven is more about a Person than it is a place. There, we will see Jesus face-to-face, and there, all of our deepest desires will be met in Him.

The Second Time

*"Therefore, stay awake, for you do not know
on what day your Lord is coming" (Matthew 24:42).*

Adapted from *The Quiet Place*, a devotional by Nancy DeMoss Wolgemuth

Christ came the first time as an infant, tiny and frail. He will return as King, great in power and glory.

He came the first time as the Lamb of God; when He returns, it will be as the Lion of the tribe of Judah.

When He came the first time, his glory was veiled and hidden from human view; when He comes the second time, His glory will shine blindingly bright.

His first coming was concealed, witnessed by a few shepherds. At His second coming, every eye will see Him, and all will know who He is.

When He came the first time only a few bowed their knee in admiration and worship; when He returns, every knee will bow, and every tongue confess that Jesus Christ is Lord.

The first time, He washed the disciple's feet; when He returns, all His enemies will be under His feet.

The first time He came, He wore a crown of thorns; when He returns, He will be crowned with many crowns, the King upon His throne.

He came the first time as our suffering Savior; He will return as our sovereign, reigning Lord.

Come quickly, Lord Jesus!

Works Cited

Wolgemuth, Nancy, Demoss. *The Quiet Place, Daily Devotional Readings.* Moody Publishers, 2012.

Chole. Alicia, Britt. *Anonymous, Jesus' hidden years and yours.* Thomas Nelson, Inc., 2006.

Assaf, Andrea, Kirk; Leahy, Kelly Anne. Compiled by. *C. S. Lewis' Little Book of Wisdom.* Hampton Roads Publishing Company, Inc., 2018.

Alcorn, Randy. March 21, 2010. *What does Romans 8:28 Really Mean?* Eternal Perspective Ministries. https://www.epm.org/resources/2010/Mar/21/romans-828-what-does-it-really-mean/

Blackaby, Henry, T; Blackaby, Richard; King, Claude, V. *Experiencing God: Knowing and Doing the Will of God.* B&H Publishing Group, 2008

Perea, Ayesh. February 13, 2024. *Hawthorne Effect: Definition, How It Works, How It Works, And How To Avoid It.* SimplyPsychology. https://www.simplypsychology.org/hawthorne-effect.html

Lazar, Shawn. February 21, 2020. *The Effects of Reading the Bible Four Times a Week.* IGES. https://faithalone.org/blog/the-effects-of-reading-the-bible-four-days-a-week/

Milbrod, Mark. June 2, 2020. *Gentlemen, This is a Football!!.* Agent Support Group. https://asglife.com/gentlemen-this-is-a-football/

The Treasure You Already Have. Day 30. http://www.graceimmersion.com/day30

Columbia, David, Patrick. November 27, 2019. *Hetty Green: The Woman Who Loved Money.* New York Social Diary. https://www.newyorksocialdiary.com/the-woman-who-loved-money/

Brettschneider, Martha. October 6, 2018. *Redwoods, Roots, and the Power of Connection.* https://damselwings.com/2018/10/06/redwoods-roots-power-of-connection/

Cagney, Mary. 1998. *Patrick The Saint.* Christian History Institute. https://christianhistoryinstitute.org/magazine/article/patrick-the-saint

Panagiotidi, Dr. Maria. October 20, 2021. *The Attention Span Myth, UX Psychology.* https://uxpsychology.substack.com/p/the-attention-span-myth

Newell, Lloyd. *The Touching Story Behind "It is Well With My Soul". The Tabernacle Choir.* https://www.thetabernaclechoir.org/articles/it-is-well-with-my-soul.html?lang=eng

Bradbury, Woodman. *Fanny Crosby. Wholesome Words Home.* https://www.wholesomewords.org/biography/bcrosby8.html

Friends, Joni and. *Our History.* https://joniandfriends.org/about/our-history/

Hagen, Carrie. December 9, 2015. *The 'Charlie Brown Christmas' Special Was The Flop That Wasn't. Smithsonian Magazine.* https://www.smithsonianmag.com/history/charlie-brown-christmas-special-history-television-classic-cbs-180957490/

Printed in the USA
CPSIA information can be obtained
at www.ICGtesting.com
CBHW061921110324
5209CB00004B/10